Shōbōgenzō

Shōbōgenzō

Zen Essays by Dōgen

TRANSLATED BY
THOMAS CLEARY

University of Hawaii Press
Honolulu

93 94 95 96 97   5 4 3 2

Library of Congress Cataloging-in-Publication Data

Dōgen, 1200–1253.
  Shōbōgenzō, Zen essays.

  Includes bibliography.
  1. Sōtōshū—Doctrines—Early works to 1800.
I. Cleary, Thomas F., 1949–   . II. Title.
III. Title: Zen essays.
BQ9449.D654S532   1986   294.3'85   85–20979
ISBN 0–8248–1014–7
ISBN 0–8248–1401–0 (pbk)

University of Hawaii Press books are printed on acid-free paper and
meet the guidelines for permanence and durability of the Council on
Library Resources

Contents

Foreword

The thirteenth-century Japanese Zen teacher Dōgen Kigen is widely respected as a religious reformer, an accomplished Buddhist adept, a profound thinker, and a brilliant writer. His master work, *Shōbōgenzō*, written in a complex, innovative style, appreciated in recent times not only for its philosophical achievements but even for its literary excellence, is among the most demanding of Zen texts. Acting forcefully on the inertia of routine thought, the *Shōbōgenzō* demonstrates how the mind is used in working Zen, and how literature can be used to foster and direct the Zen use of the mind. This volume presents translations of thirteen chapters of the *Shōbōgenzō*, selected for their emphasis on perennial issues in Buddhist learning and action.

Introduction

Zen Master Dōgen is revered as the founder of the Sōtō Zen school in Japan, but in modern times his reputation as an exceptionally advanced intellect has reached far beyond sectarian bounds. Largely kept hidden for centuries, Dōgen's *Shōbōgenzō*, a remarkable collection of essays, has lately attracted widespread attention from scholars and others within and without Zen circles. Much admired for its linguistic artistry and metaphysical subtlety, the *Shōbōgenzō* is a classic of such status and magnitude that entire careers have been devoted to its study and exegesis.

According to the *Kenzeiki*, a medieval biography of Dōgen,[1] the master was born in the year 1200 C.E. to a noble family in Kyoto, the imperial capital and cultural center of Japan. While still a small child he began to receive the rigorous education considered proper for his status and expectations, learning classical Chinese, the language of philosophy and government in old Japan. At the age of seven he was already reading the ancient Chinese classics *Tso Chuan* and *Mao Shih* and was considered a prodigy by Confucian scholars of the time.

When Dōgen was eight his mother died. This event is said to have awakened him to the impermanence of life and provoked in him a desire to leave secular society and become a monk. Later, when he finally left home and abandoned his future at court, he revealed that his dying mother had herself urged him to become a monk. He began to add Buddhist lore to the enormous stock of book learning which he accumulated over the years, and is said to have been reading intricate Buddhist *abhidharma*, analytic philosophy, by the age of nine.

About this time, Dōgen was adopted by the imperial regent, a distinguished scholar and statesman, and was taught political science as it was known at that time, with a view to making him a member of the court. Dōgen, however, had no desire for a secular career and at the age of thirteen ran away to become a monk. He sought out an uncle who was a high priest of the Tendai school of Buddhism, and prevailed upon him to accept his decision to leave home and help him to attain his wish to pursue a religious life.

At fourteen Dōgen was formally ordained and "studied the way of the Tendai school, including the secret teachings from south India, the principles of the greater and lesser vehicles, and the inner meanings of the exoteric and esoteric doctrines." When he was fifteen he went to see the Zen master Eisai and heard about the teachings of the Rinzai school of Zen; the following year Eisai died, and Dōgen continued to consult his successor Myōzen, seeing the latter on and off for several years until he finally became his disciple formally when he was eighteen years old. During this time Dōgen also continued his canonical studies and is said to have read through the whole of the voluminous Buddhist canon twice while still in his teens.

Dōgen is said to have been encouraged to study Zen by a high priest of the Tendai school to whom he applied with his question of why Buddhas aspire to and practice the way of enlightenment if the reality of enlightenment is inherent. According to *Denkōroku,* another medieval Sōtō text, Dōgen under Myōzen's tutelage studied not only Zen but also ethical precepts, the Tendai meditation methods known as "stopping and seeing" *(shi-kan),* and esoteric rites, in the manner of Eisai's syncretic school. When Dōgen was twenty-one he was given recognition as Myōzen's Zen successor, and was thus considered a tenth-generation heir of the Ōryū branch of Rinzai Zen, which Eisai had introduced from China.

By his own account, Dōgen studied with Myōzen for nine years. At the age of twenty-four he went to China with Myōzen for further inquiry. The political conditions in China at that time made it impractical, if not impossible, to travel widely, but Dōgen was able to meet several Zen teachers in eastern China. After fruitless contact with seven Zen teachers, however, he felt he had nothing to learn from any of them and decided to return to Japan. He was urged, however, to see the redoubtable Nyojō, who had just replaced the late abbot of a famous public monastery. In 1225 Dōgen met the man who was to be his last teacher.

Absorbed in learning and meditating, Dōgen spent nearly two years in the congregation of Nyojō without ever lying down to sleep. Finally, one morning in the early hours he heard the teacher scold a dozing monk with the words, "Zen study requires the shedding of body and mind," and at that moment Dōgen was greatly awakened. Subsequently his realization was recognized by Nyojō, and he was formally designated a successor. In 1227, having, in his own words, "finished his life's study," Dōgen returned to Japan.

In Japan Dōgen did not hasten to set himself up as a teacher. He stayed for a time at Kenninji, the monastery in Kyoto founded by Eisai at which he had studied with Eisai's successor Myōzen. According to *Denkōroku,* over the next few years Dōgen spent time at thirteen different places offered to him by patrons, but none of them suited him. In 1234 he settled down at Kōshō Hōrin temple outside Kyoto and began to teach. The *Denkōroku* states that more than fifty students gathered here, including Koun Ejō, who was to become Dōgen's first successor.

In 1235 Ejō was formally installed as the assembly leader and recognized as Dōgen's heir and teaching assistant. That same year Dōgen began to solicit funds to build a monks' hall *(sōdō),* used for communal meditation and residence in a traditional Zen monastery. Dōgen was the first Japanese Zen teacher to base his organization on the observances of Chinese Zen without the admixture of rites from the esoteric branch of Tendai Buddhism that had characterized the organization of Eisai and Myōzen.

Something of the historical sense that Dōgen had of his transmission of Zen to Japan can be glimpsed in a 1242 conversation with a nobleman who asked if the Zen school had been transmitted to Japan in past times. Dōgen replied:

> In our country literal and formal Buddhism has been transmitted, and it has been somewhat more than four hundred years that the terms and forms of Buddhism have been heard of here. And now the Buddha-mind school (Zen) is becoming current: and it should be at precisely this time.
>
> In China literal and formal Buddhism was first transmitted between 58 and 76 C.E.; from then to the year 520 (when Bodhidharma brought Zen from India to China) is somewhat more than four hundred years. It was at that time that the way of the adepts, direct pointing, brought from the West (India), first became current. Six generations later was Sokei (the sixth patriarch of Zen in China), and after (his disciples) Seigen and Nangaku it branched into five schools.
>
> In our country nominal Buddhism was first heard of in the sixth century C.E., after which the sacred doctrines transmitted from Korea filled the land. But there have not yet been adepts at transmitting mind by mind— there has only been a succession of nation-protecting and wonder-working monks.[2]

Since it was more than four hundred years between the time of the first introduction of Buddhism into Japan and Dōgen's bringing of Zen from China, it is likely that Dōgen's reckoning refers to the founding of the Tendai and Shingon schools in the early ninth century, which would be four centuries before Dōgen brought Zen, referred to here by the traditional terms "direct pointing," "the way of the adepts," and "transmitting mind by mind." So-called "nation-protecting and wonder-working monks" refers to the practice of rites for the protection of the state and production of magical effects, known to be prevalent in Japanese Buddhism of the time. Basically, Dōgen relates the transmission of Zen by analogy to Chinese Buddhist history, suggesting that the time in Japan was finally ripe to progress from the externals of Buddhism, the names and forms, to the internal, mind-to-mind transmission. Although Dōgen declined to use the term "Zen sect," emphasizing the essential unity of Buddhism, the evidence suggests that he was aware of initiating something new in the history of Japanese Buddhism.

In 1242, one of his most prolific years in terms of the composition of *Shōbōgenzō*, Dōgen formally designated his second successor, Gi'in. In the same year, the monk Shinchi Kakushin came to Dōgen and received the Mahayana Buddhist precepts from him. This monk later went to China and succeeded to the teaching of Mumon Ekai, author of the popular Zen classic *Mumonkan;* he eventually returned to Japan, beginning his own Zen school, and was given the honorific title Lamp of Religion, Teacher of the Nation. Also in 1242, the recorded sayings of Dōgen's teacher Nyojō arrived from China.

During his decade or so at Kōshō temple, Dōgen had many contacts with the nobility of Kyoto and initiated over two thousand people into the bodhisattva precepts. Finally he came to desire a more quiet and undisturbed setting. The *Kenzeiki* records that he was offered twelve different places by patrons, none of which suited him—a possible reference to the same process mentioned in *Denkōroku,* which says that Dōgen was offered thirteen places from the time he came back to Japan until the time he settled at Kōshō. In any case, Dōgen was finally offered an old temple site in the province of Echizen, modern Fukui prefecture, by the provincial governor at whose residence Dōgen had delivered the *Shōbōgenzō* essay *Zenki* in 1242. Dōgen accepted this offer and in 1243 took up residence in Echizen. In 1244 he formally opened his new monastery, then called Daibutsuji; in 1246 its name was changed to Eiheiji, as it is known today.

During the 1240s Dōgen was given a robe and title of honor by the emperor Gosaga. This period was most productive. He wrote nearly eighty of the ninety-five essays of the *Shōbōgenzō* between 1239 and 1246, the majority of them between 1240 and 1243.

In 1247, invited by the regent of the military government, Hōjō Tokiyori, an earnest Zen student, and also urged by his patron the governor of Echizen, Dōgen went to Kamakura in eastern Japan, the seat of the shogunate. Tokiyori wanted Dōgen to stay in Kamakura and offered him the position of founding abbot of the new Kenchōji monastery, but Dōgen refused and returned to Eiheiji after six months in Kamakura. Upon his return he said these words in a speech to his disciples:

> Last year on the third day of the eighth month I left the mountain and went to Kamakura and expounded the Teaching for a patron lay disciple. This year, this month, yesterday, I returned, and this morning I have come before you to speak. Some people may be suspicious about this event. I crossed so many mountains and rivers to expound the Teaching for a lay disciple—this seems like esteeming a layman more than monks. Also some may wonder if there is a teaching I have not explained here, a teaching you have not heard. But there is no teaching I have not explained here, none you have not heard. I only explained to him that those who do good rise while those who do evil fall. Cultivating cause, effect is experienced.[3]

He ended the speech with the remark that his love of the mountains was even greater than before, and this theme of retreat and seclusion from secular society, which appears elsewhere in his works, gains increasing emphasis toward the end of Dōgen's life.

In the same year, 1247, Dōgen also exchanged correspondence with Zen Master Daikaku (Rankei Dōryū), a Chinese Zen monk in Kamakura who received the post of abbot at Kenchōji which Dōgen is said to have declined. This seems to be the only clear record of contact between Dōgen and another Zen school in Japan, apart from the school founded by Eisai and the Bodhidharma sect, a native Japanese Zen movement.

In 1253 Dōgen's successor Ejō was installed as the second abbot of Eiheiji. Dōgen himself, terminally ill, went to Kyoto for medical care. Staying in the house of a lay disciple in Kyoto, Dōgen passed away in the eighth month of the same year.

Dōgen's magnum opus *Shōbōgenzō*, "Treasury of the Eye of True Teaching," is the first major Buddhist text to have been composed in the Japanese language, written in a time when classical Chinese was considered the preferred medium for religious literature in Japan, much in the same way that Latin and Arabic were the standard languages for philosophical discourse in medieval Europe. *Shōbōgenzō* contains many passages and phrases in Chinese embedded in the Japanese matrix of the text and manipulated with striking effect, producing an intense style which demands a great deal of concentration on the part of the reader. It may be said that the form as well as the content of the compositions in *Shōbōgenzō* is instrumental, in that it provokes definite effects on the attention and stream of consciousness of the reader.

Insofar as it deals with both topical and perennial matters, *Shōbōgenzō* contains material which is primarily relevant to thirteenth-century Japanese Buddhism, particularly in its monastic forms, and also material which is timeless, presenting insights that not only permeate spiritual teachings found all over the world but also anticipate modern scientific realizations about the nature of knowledge. While in certain respects Dōgen's presentations in *Shōbōgenzō* differ in manner from other Zen teachings, he also uses traditional strategies in his handling of Zen and Buddhist lore.

One characteristic which *Shōbōgenzō* shares with other Zen writing is the way Dōgen draws freely from Buddhist literature without concern for any context but that in which he is presently handling a story, saying, or technical term. This freedom includes the practice of partial quotation, using only so much of a given story or speech as is useful in conveying the intended message or impact of the moment. This practice seems to reflect the general Zen view of literature as being instrumental rather than sacred writ, allowing for a flexible exercise of possibilities in association and imagery.

Another feature of Dōgen's treatment of sayings and stories which is also to be found throughout Zen literature as an important device is referred to by Dōgen himself, and in earlier Zen writing such as the *Blue Cliff Record,* as "presenting sideways and using upside down." This is the practice of using a story, saying, term, or symbol in a way that departs from the obvious or the stereotyped, traditional view. This practice is exercised, according to Zen writing on the subject, to help break up the "nest of cliché" which Zen teaching often cites as both a symptom and a cause of mental stagnation. Apart from clichéd understanding acquired at second hand, however, even understanding which is valid at a given level of personal development inhibits deeper realization if it is held fast to as ultimate. In Buddhism this is technically called "the barrier of knowledge," and the fact that Dōgen's disciples already had considerable learning is a likely reason for Dōgen's striking use of verbal shock techniques such as this one.

A particular aspect of the barrier of knowledge which another feature of Zen literature is designed to counter is the overestimation of conceptual understanding at the expense of practical understanding. According to Zen teaching, the study of Zen requires actual participation, because it is only through participation that the transformation of the individual can take place. Zen literature does not merely state this principle, however; it enforces it, so to speak, by presenting material that is impenetrable without the exercise of qualities essential to Zen work, such as patience, concentration, and ability to suspend automatic thought.

Confucius, the great educator of ancient China, reportedly said that if he pointed out one corner of a matter and the student could not come back with the other three, he would not repeat himself. This statement by Confucius is cited in classic Zen writing to indicate that the capacity to "understand three when one is raised" is also essential in Zen students. The principle of "not saying everything" or "not explaining thoroughly" *(fuseppa)* so as to provoke the student to the necessary levels of effort is found explicitly and implicitly in many forms in Zen literature, and is also applied by Dōgen in *Shōbōgenzō*. One of Dōgen's characteristic devices is to present a number of views, often generating them from variations on themes from stories and sayings, then leaving the audience to work through them. Sometimes this is done in the form of a series of questions which Dōgen then tells his hearers to think over.

Emphasis on concentration techniques is a common feature of the three "new" or "reform" movements of Japanese Buddhism in Dōgen's time—the Nichiren, Pure Land, and Zen schools. Close study of the literature of each of these forms of Buddhism reveals a demand for concentration in conjunction with special attention patterns, concrete methods of developing concentration, and a wealth of concealed meanings which are only accessible in the light of structured concentration. Concentration is deemed necessary to empower the teachings, to validate them experientially, because existing mental habits, which form boundaries inhibiting the potential of consciousness of the conditioned person, go back to "beginningless time"—that is, to subconscious sociopersonal history—and have become ingrained or "naturalized" into the fabric of the person's views of reality. Conceptual exercise alone is held to be too shallow and ephemeral to exert the force necessary to break through deeply established mental conditionings. The "doubt feeling" (gijō), deliberately produced by certain Zen verbal devices frustrating linear thought, is one way in which such force is accumulated and directed in order to pierce this veil of inertia.

Much of Dōgen's writing in Shōbōgenzō dealing with perennial issues may be read on both philosophical and experiential planes, as indeed these planes mirror one another. The actual integration of these realms of understanding, however, takes place after the Zen initiatory experience (nissho), which uproots the fixation of views and makes possible the more subtle perceptions and integrations with which more advanced Zen practice works. In systematic Zen kōan study, at least as it is represented in the writings of Sung dynasty Chinese teachers and Japanese teachers, simple kōan which focus the attention off of discriminating consciousness on to totality are dealt with first, to break conceptual habits. After gross fixations of conditioned thought are shed and a measure of flexibility is retrieved, more complex kōan are taken up in order to integrate holistic and differentiating awareness. A great deal of Dōgen's writings for contemplation in Shōbōgenzō would fall into the general category of complex kōan, and can be used with great effect in aiding the mind in the practice of fluid integration of multiple perspectives.

To appreciate this quality of Shōbōgenzō, it is helpful to have a glimpse of the practical core of which the Shōbōgenzō meditations are refinements. Observation of certain fundamentals of Zen meditation will also afford a rough comparison of Dōgen's approaches with those of other teachers.

Certain basic patterns can be discerned in expressions of Zen meditation techniques designed to bring about transformation of consciousness. For example, a recurrent image in Zen literature is that of death and rebirth, referring to the process of stripping away the accretions of conditioning and then returning to the ordinary world purified and free. An analogy may be drawn with the famous line of scripture which says "form is empty, emptiness is form"; experientially, "form is empty" corresponds to detachment from appearances, while "emptiness is form" corresponds to the fullness of the field of perception accessible to the opened mind. This twin aspect of enlightenment experience is also referred to by such terms as "the heart of nirvana and the knowledge of differentiation," "silence and illumination," "dismantling and constructing," and a host of similarly structured metaphors.

Sōzan, one of the early masters of the Sōtō Zen tradition, expresses this process in the following terms: "As a beginner, knowing there is something fundamental in oneself, when one turns the light around (shifts attention from sense experience to the essence of mind) one ejects form, sound, smell, flavor, touch, and phenomena, and attains tranquility. Then, after fully accomplishing this, one does not grasp the sense data but descends among them without being blinded, letting them be, without interference."[4]

Dōgen's teacher Nyojō provides a vivid description along similar lines:

> You should "gouge out" your eyes and see nothing at all—after that there will be nothing you don't see; only then can it be called seeing. . . . You should "block off" your ears and hear nothing at all—after that there will be nothing you don't hear; only then can it be called hearing. . . . You should "knock off" your nose and not distinguish smells—after that there will be none you can't distinguish; only then can it be called smelling. . . . You should "pull out" your tongue, so that the world is silent—after that your ebullience will be uninterrupted; only then can it be called speaking. . . . You should "slough off" the physical elements and be completely independent—after that you manifest forms adapting to various types; only then can it be called person. . . . You should permanently stop clinging thought, so the incalculable ages are empty—after that arising and vanishing continue unceasing; only then can it be called consciousness.[5]

In an early treatise on *zazen*, Dōgen says, "You should stop the intellectual practice of pursuing words and learn the 'stepping back' of 'turning the light around and shining back'; mind and body will naturally 'drop off,' and the 'original face' will appear." The Zen "art" of looking into the mind source instead of pursuing thoughts or external stimuli is called *ekō henshō*, "turning the light around and shining (or looking) back." In this same treatise, and in *Shōbōgenzō*, Dōgen uses the following story to illustrate the method of this practice, which he calls the essential art of *zazen*. As the Zen master Yakuzan was sitting, a monk asked, "What are you thinking of, so still and intent." Yakuzan said, "I am thinking of that which is not thinking." The monk said, "How can one think of that which is not thinking." Yakuzan said, "It isn't thought."⁶ In his *Zazenshin* essay in *Shōbōgenzō*, Dōgen writes, "In thinking of *what isn't thinking,* one always uses *nonthought*. In *nonthought* is 'who'—'who' carries 'I'."⁷

The word "who," or some phrase like "who is carrying around this corpse?" is also one of the "words" *(watō)* that have been traditionally used in Zen meditation (particularly since the late Sung dynasty) to evoke the "doubt feeling" *(gijō)* of looking into the innermost self. There are numerous sayings and stories in the records of the classical Zen masters alluding to this practice of "looking back." A monk once asked Master Isan, "What is the Path?" Isan said, "No-mind is the Path." The monk said, "I don't understand." Isan said, "You should understand that which doesn't understand." The monk asked, "What is that which doesn't understand?" Isan said, "Just you are it. It is not someone else." Isan continued, "People of the present time should just directly realize that which doesn't understand. This indeed is your mind, this indeed is your Buddha. If you externally get a piece of knowledge, a piece of understanding, and consider that the path of Zen, you're out of touch. This is called carrying excrement in—it is not called taking excrement out. It defiles your mind-field, so I say it is not the Path."⁸

Gyōzan asked Isan, "What is the abode of the real Buddha?" Isan said, "With the subtlety of thinking of no thought, think back to the endlessness of the spiritual flame. When thought is exhausted, you return to the source; essence and characteristics always abide, phenomena and noumenon are not two—the real Buddha is thusness as is."⁹

A monk asked the adept Shijō, "Whenever I sit at night, my thoughts are in a flurry, and I don't know how to subdue them. Please give me some guidance." Shijō said:

> When you sit still at night and your thoughts are in a flurry, then use the flurried mind to investigate the place of the flurry. Investigating this thoroughly, you find there is no place—then how can the flurry of thoughts remain? Then turn back to investigate the investigating mind—then where

is the mind which can investigate? Furthermore, the perceiving knowledge is fundamentally empty, so the object focused on is also quiescent. Quiescent yet not quiescent, because there is no stilling person; perceiving yet not perceiving, because there is no perceived object. When object and knowledge are both quiescent, mind and thought are at rest. Outwardly not pursuing ramifications, inwardly not dwelling in concentration, both roads having disappeared, the one nature is tranquil. This is the essential path of returning to the source.[10]

This technique is also part of the battery of meditation practices of Tendai Buddhism. For example, one meditation manual says, "Since we know observation comes from mind, or from analyzing objects, this is not merging with the fundamental source: so one should turn back to observe the observing mind."[11] This type of introspection is also found in the technical literature of the Pure Land school in China:

Outwardly not clinging to objects, inwardly not dwelling in concentration, "turn the light around" and observe once—inside and outside are both quiescent. After that subtly invoke the name of Amitabhā Buddha three to five times. Turn the light around and introspect—"it is said that seeing nature one realizes buddhahood; ultimately, what is my inherent Amitabhā Buddha?" Then also watch and observe that which has just brought this up— "where does this one thought come from?" Seeing through this one thought, then see through this seer—who is it?[12]

A useful Zen story illustrating the technique of "turning the light around and looking back"—its application and limitations—is found in the *Book of Serenity* (in Japanese, *Shōyōroku*), a classic collection of Zen lore compiled and expounded by outstanding Chinese Sōtō Zen masters. The master Gyōzan asked a monk, "Where do you come from?" The monk said, "From Yun-chou." Gyōzan said, "Do you think of that place?" The monk said, "I always think of it." Gyōzan said, "That which thinks is mind, that which is thought of is object. In that place are various things—mountains, rivers, land, buildings, houses, people, animals. Think back to the mind which thinks—are there so many things in there?" The monk said, "When I get here, I do not see their existence at all." Gyōzan said, "This is right for the stage of faith, but not yet for the stage of person."

Basically, in this technique the exercise is to turn away from the preoccupations of the mind and back to the mind itself. Since mind or awareness as an object in itself cannot be grasped, the exercise of focus on an ungraspable object, or objectless focus, has a particular effect. The teacher says that the monk's state of disentanglement from objects and absorption in the objectless mind is right for the stage of "faith." In Zen literature, the expression "entry by faith" appears occasionally in reference to an initial stage of enlightenment. Faith here does not mean belief in an idea or object; rather it has the sense of acquiescence. The Zen master Rinzai refers to insufficient faith or "trust" in oneself as the reason for restless external search and the consequent failure to realize intrinsic enlightenment.

In the aforementioned treatise on meditation, Dōgen also writes, "Even if one can boast of understanding, is rich in enlightenment, gains a glimpse of penetrating knowledge, attains the Way, clarifies the mind, and becomes very high spirited, yet even though one roams freely within the bounds of 'entry,' one may lack the living road of manifestation in being." Here what is referred to as "entry," a common Zen term for initiation into enlightened consciousness, might be equated with what Gyōzan refers to as the "stage of faith" in the foregoing story, while Gyōzan's stage of "person" might be equated with what Dōgen refers to, using a familiar Zen expression, as the "living road of manifestation in being," a step beyond preliminary disentanglement from objects.

The story goes on. The monk asked, "Do you have any other particular directions?" Gyōzan said, "To say there is something particular or not would not be accurate. Based on your view, you only get one mystery. You get the seat and wear the robe—after this, see on your own." If one applies the model of the "seat," "robe," and "room" of Buddha according to the *Hokke (Saddharmapuṇḍarīka)* scripture, the "seat" is the emptiness of all phenomena, the "robe" is forbearance. These fit the story rather well, considering that the effect of the exercise of looking into the mind is disentanglement. The "room" of a Buddha is compassion, and this is the essence of being in the world, of active expression; this also fits the story as well as Dōgen's admonition, representing the next stage of development.

The poem recorded in the *Book of Serenity* illustrating this story, composed by Wanshi, acknowledged as one of the great masters of Sōtō Zen, clarifies these points most beautifully: "Containing without omission, penetrating without obstruction. Gates and walls high and steep, barrier locks doubled and redoubled. The wine always sweet, it lays out the guests; though the meal is filling, it ruins the farmers. The wind supports the condor's wings as it bursts out in space; thunder accompanies the dragon as it treads over the ocean."

"Containing without omission, penetrating without obstruction" characterizes the mind; "gates and walls high and steep, barrier locks doubled and redoubled" characterizes objects. "The wine always sweet, it lays out the guests; though the meal is filling, it ruins the farmers"—this refers to absorption in mind-introspection; total indulgence in this at the expense of participation in the world produces a lopsided, partial development. In Buddhist scriptures concentration is sometimes referred to as "wine," meditation as "food"—indulgence in "intoxication" and "tasting" is forbidden to the bodhisattvas, who are to balance detachment and identification, transcendence and being in the world. Here being in the world, the active personality, is symbolized by "guest" and "farmer," and this is seen as a necessary part of the total balance of the whole being.

"The wind supports the condor's wings as it bursts out in space; thunder accompanies the dragon as it treads over the ocean." Here the "condor" and "dragon" represent the awakened person; the "wind" and "thunder" refer to the world, which becomes a vehicle for the awakened. The phrase "bursts out in space," which can be taken to refer to emancipation, emptying, can also be read "bursts out of empty space," suggesting going beyond the stage of emptiness. The phrase "treads over the ocean" is literally "treads on and turns over the ocean," conveying a similar sense of going beyond the oceanic realm of pure consciousness. So in the end the exercise of "turning the light around and looking back" can be seen as a means of "entry," to be replaced by a more comprehensive realization of integration. An ancient teacher said, "If you haven't attained entry, first attain entry; if you have attained entry, don't turn your back on me," suggesting again that there is more to learn after awakening.

Accordingly, Dōgen describes this technique as "the essential art of *zazen*" but does not refer to it as the whole art of *zazen*. Clearly, there is more content in the total program of meditation in Zen schools, and a function of the teacher's contact with the students is to provide material for contemplation. Dōgen's *Shōbōgenzō* provides numerous examples of outlines for meditations presented to his disciples to work through, and he repeatedly urges them to ponder his questions and statements carefully.

It is well known that in the Rinzai Zen schools *kōan*, Zen stories, are commonly used in meditation, with pressure being put on the student to "answer" or illustrate the *kōan* as part of the method. Since there are many cases in Dōgen's written and spoken works where he deals with traditional *kōan*, and also evidence of his own use of *kōan* as a testing device, there can be no doubt that the *kōan* was an integral part of his teaching method. Nevertheless, it is questionable whether Dōgen gave the *kōan* the same kind of stress as Rinzai Zen teachers ordinarily did, or similarly demanded answers in a graded system. In a record of some of his early teaching, he seems to play down the value of such a method:

> In the study of the Way, the prime essential is sitting meditation *(zazen)*. The attainment of the Way by numerous people in China is due in each case to the power of sitting meditation. Even ignorant people with no talent, who do not understand a single letter, if they sit wholeheartedly in meditation, then by the accomplishment of meditative stability they will surpass even brilliant people who have studied for a long time. Thus, students should only be concerned with the act of sitting—do not get involved with other things. The Way of Buddhas is just sitting meditation; one should not follow other concerns.
>
> (Ejō asked,) In practicing both sitting and reading, when looking at the recorded sayings (of Zen masters) and *kōan*, it happens that one may understand somewhat one out of a hundred or a thousand. In the case of sitting meditation, there is no particular experiential proof such as this. Yet should we still be devoted to sitting meditation?
>
> (Dōgen replied,) When looking at the words of the public cases, though one may seem to have some perception, that is a factor which causes estrangement from the Way of Buddhas. If you spend your time sitting straight without attaining anything or understanding anything, then it would be the Way of Buddhas. Although even the ancients encouraged both reading and just sitting, they still encouraged sitting wholeheartedly. And though there have been people whose awakening was opened by words, those too were situations in which the opening of awakening was due to the accomplishment in sitting. The true attainment is due to the sitting.[13]

However, in the same record there is also evidence that contemplating sayings was practiced in Dōgen's school:

It is said, "Even a thousand acres of clear fields is not as good as a bit of skill that you can take around with you." "Benevolence does not hope for reward; having given to someone, do not regret it." "If you keep your mouth as silent as your nose, you will avoid ten thousand calamities." "A person whose action is firm is naturally admired; but someone of outstanding ability will naturally be brought down." "To plow deep but plant shallow is the way to a natural disaster. When you help yourself and harm others, how could there be no consequences?" When students of the Way are looking at sayings, you must exert your power to the utmost and examine them very very closely.[14]

It is interesting to note that the specific examples Dōgen mentions in this speech are not of the type usually associated with *kōan* meditation, but rather appear on the surface as advice for living. In other works of Dōgen there are *kōan* with his comments in prose and poetry in traditional Zen style.

In connection with practice, Dōgen is noted for asserting the unity of practice and realization. In one of his early essays, *Bendōwa,* he writes:

To think practice and realization are not one is a heretical view. In Buddhism, practice and realization are one equivalence. Even now, because it is practice based on realization, the beginner's practice of the Way is the whole of the fundamental realization. For this reason, even in presenting the orientation of practice, the teaching is to not anticipate realization outside of practice; this must be because it is the fundamental realization, directly pointed to. Being the realization of practice, there is no boundary of realization; being the practice of realization, there is no beginning of practice. . . . Since there is practice which is not apart from realization, the beginner's practice of the Way, in which we are fortunate to simply transmit one portion of subtle practice, is precisely attainment of one portion of fundamental realization in the state of nonstriving. You should know that the enlightened ones repeatedly teach that practice should not be relaxed, so that realization which is not apart from practice will not be defiled. When you put down subtle practice, fundamental realization fills your hands; when you express fundamental realization bodily, subtle practice is carried out through your whole body.[15]

This approach of presenting practice as "practice of realization" and realization as "realization of practice" may be further clarified in terms of the Tendai doctrine of the six aspects of identity between conscious beings and Buddha—identity in respect to essence, doctrine, meditation practice, conformity, partial realization, and ultimate realization. As Dōgen says, practice is practice of realization, so it must first of all be based on the essence, the intrinsic buddha-nature; recollecting this essence and cultivating its expression in action, however, generally depend on teaching to point the way. Insofar as meditation practice is attuned to the true essence by way of teaching and correct application, it can develop into conformity with the essence. By purification of the senses and conformity with the essence, the veil of ignorance—the habit energy of the ego—is removed, and the essence, the buddha-nature or original mind, then takes over the consciousness and ultimately becomes fully awakened and manifest in life. From the beginning the essence is the same, while the depth of realization of it on the part of the person corresponds to the degree of purity and perfection of practical conformity with it and expression of it.

Dōgen's presentation of *zazen* practice is at times also reminiscent of the teaching of esoteric Buddhism of the Shingon school and the esoteric branch of the Tendai school, according to which the unity of the cosmic Buddha and all existence is realized and expressed in people through the medium of certain physical, verbal, and mental actions. In the case of the esoteric rites, these would be the various *mudrā* (symbolic gestures or signs), *mantra* or *dhāraṇī* (mystic incantations), and *samādhi* (concentration, absorption in specific visualizations and thoughts). In *Bendōwa* Dōgen writes, "If someone, even for one period of time, shows the Buddha-seal in physical, verbal, and mental action, and sits straight in concentration, the whole cosmos becomes the Buddha-seal, all of space becomes enlightenment."[16]

There is, however, a stipulation: the ego must be overcome. In the *Genjōkōan* essay in *Shōbōgenzō* Dōgen writes that ego-laden practice and realization are delusion; as long as there is egotism—attachment to the idea of the self—practice and realization cannot be practice and realization of enlightenment. In one of his early talks Dōgen makes this clear, and also recommends a traditional method for overcoming this barrier:

> The foremost concern of a student is first to detach from the notion of self. To detach from the notion of self means that we must not cling to this body. Even if you have thoroughly studied the stories of the ancients and sit constantly like iron or stone, if you are attached to your body and do not

detach from it, you could not find the Way of Buddhas even in ten thousand eons, in a thousand lifetimes. Though you may say you have understood the temporary and true doctrines and the true exoteric and esoteric teachings, if you do not leave off your feeling of attachment to your body, you are idly counting the treasures of others without having a halfpenny of your own. I only ask that students sit quietly and look into the beginning and end of this body as it truly is. The body, limbs, hair, and skin come from the sperm and ovum; when the breath ceases, they separate and decay in the mountains and fields, eventually turning into mud and earth. What do you have to cling to as your body? This is all the more apparent when we look at it from the point of view of the elements; in the conjunction and dispersal of the elements, what elements can you definitely consider as your own body? Whether it is within the teachings (i.e. doctrinal schools) or outside the teachings (i.e. Zen schools), the fact is the same—that neither beginning nor end of one's body can be grasped is the essential point to be aware of in practicing the Way. If you have first arrived at this truth, the real Buddha Way is something that is obviously so.[17]

Attachment to self also has more subtle manifestations, and Dōgen distinguishes the *zazen* of non-Buddhists and Buddhists aiming for individual salvation from the *zazen* of Buddhas in terms of characteristic flaws which are related to some sense of self. Quoting the great Buddhist master Nāgārjuna, Dōgen says that the *zazen* of non-Buddhists has the flaw of attachment to experiences and wrong views, while the *zazen* of Buddhists in quest of individual salvation has the flaw of aspiration for self-tranquilization and aiming for extinction.[18] A similar sense of clinging being a barrier to true realization is expressed in the *Sandhinirmocana* scripture in explaining the relationship between practices and ultimate truth.

According to the argument of this scripture, if ultimate truth and practices were entirely the same, then everyone, regardless of what they do, would have seen the truth and would have attained nirvana or enlightenment; but since not everyone has actually seen the truth and attained nirvana or enlightenment, it cannot be said that ultimate truth and practices are entirely the same.

Furthermore, it explains, if there were no difference at all between ultimate truth and practices, then since practices are susceptible to degeneration, so also would ultimate truth be susceptible to degeneration; but whatever is subject to degeneration cannot be ultimate truth. Moreover, whereas forms of practice are differentiated, ultimate truth is undifferentiated, inasmuch as what varies is not ultimate. So again it cannot be said that ultimate truth and practices are no different.

On the other hand, the scripture continues, if ultimate truth and practices were totally different, then those who see the truth would not be able to do away with the forms of practice and would still be in bondage to form, since realization of truth would have no effect on a totally different realm. However, those who see the truth are in fact able to do away with the forms of practice, these being conditional and not absolute, and they are indeed freed from bondage to form.

The common characteristic of practices is ultimate truth, the emptiness or nonabsoluteness of forms. Viewing it from another angle, the scripture says that practices being the manifestations of selflessness is itself the characteristic of ultimate truth. Thus practices and ultimate truth cannot be said to be completely different, just as they cannot be said to be no different.

This scripture illustrates how, on the one hand, it can be said that practice and realization are one, yet on the other hand some people are said to become enlightened and others not, and some practice and realization is said to be delusion while other practice and realization is said to be enlightenment. Dōgen's critical stipulation of detachment from self is reflected in the scripture's statement that practice being a manifestation of selflessness is the characteristic of ultimate truth—under this condition they are one. Furthermore, as noted, attachment to self can mean clinging not only to the idea and feeling of self as a physical entity, but also to the experiences and aims and thoughts of the self. Here again Dōgen differentiates the enlightened and the unenlightened within fundamental realization in terms of the presence or absence of barriers such as clinging to concepts. In *Bendōwa* he writes, "The Buddhas, always herein as maintainers, do not leave conceptual knowledge on its several particular aspects; as common beings eternally function herein, its aspects do not appear in their several particular conceptual knowledges."[19] Accordingly, in another talk on *zazen*, Dōgen speaks of it as beyond any formulation or notion or experience, in conformity with the nonduality of ultimate truth and practice as described in the scripture:

> The *zazen* of the Buddhas is not motion or stillness, not practice or realization. It has nothing to do with mind or body, it doesn't depend on delusion or enlightenment. It doesn't empty mental objects, it doesn't cling to any

realm of sense. It doesn't value form, sensation, conception, conditionings, or discriminating consciousness. Study of the Way doesn't use form, sensation, conception, conditionings, or discriminating consciousness—if you act on form, sensation, conception, conditionings, or discriminating consciousness, this is form, sensation, conception, conditions, and discriminating consciousness, not study of the Way.[20]

Nonetheless, as seen in the teaching of the middle way, complete realization embraces both absolute and relative truth. Since ancient times Buddhism has noted that extremism is a characteristic disease of human thought and action, and in Zen lore it is pointed out that effort to transcend form can lapse into nihilism. Nāgārjuna wrote, "Emptiness has been said by the Conquerors (Buddhas) to be the relinquishment of views; but they have said that those who hold to the view of emptiness are incurable."[21] In a similar vein, Dōgen says, "Originally the various 'emptinesses' were needed to break through existence. Once / Since there are no existents, what 'emptiness' is needed?"[22] The principles of emptiness and meditation on emptiness are used to break through reification of phenomena as subjectively viewed; when it is actually realized that there is nothing in the world that can be grasped as permanent, definite, or absolute, and clinging to objects is ended, then "emptiness" has fulfilled its function. The fourth patriarch of Zen said, "The practice of bodhisattvas has emptiness as its realization: when beginning students see emptiness, this is seeing emptiness, it is not real emptiness. Those who cultivate the Way and attain real emptiness do not see emptiness or nonemptiness; they have no views."[23]

In spite of the clarity of such statements by Nāgārjuna and others regarding the meaning of emptiness and its function as a doctrine and a focus of meditation, there is a persistent tendency, noted in Buddhist texts over the ages, for both observers and participants to exaggerate emptiness into nihilism. Zen writings of the Sung dynasty particularly mention this as a prevalent form of immaturity or degeneracy in Zen, a typical symptom of which is denial or ignorance of cause and effect relations. Dōgen, having studied in Sung China, and working in Japan during the early period of transplantation of Sung Zen traditions, also addresses this issue in emphatic terms from a number of angles; it may even be possible to see this as a major theme of the *Shōbōgenzō,* recurring in various forms.

Dōgen's famous paraphrase of the scriptural line "all beings have buddha-nature" into "all being is buddha-nature" might be taken as representative of this effort to resolve unintegrated dualities. In his essay on buddha-nature, *Busshō,* he complains that portraying the "moon disc," which conventionally represents buddha-nature, as an empty circle is misleading, because in fact all forms and appearances are themselves the "moon disc." Here he addresses the philosophical and meditative error of imagining buddha-nature as like a soul or spirit separate from the body and distinct from the total field of experience, a realm of clarity divorced from the everyday world. Such a realm of clarity is a mental object, a state cultivated by concentration, and whatever its value as a temporary tool may be, it is not true realization of the all-embracing awareness of enlightenment.

Perhaps nowhere is Dōgen's counterbalancing of negative extremism more concisely typified than in a passage in his *Sesshin-sesshō* essay where he mentions the famous image of the "true person with no position" used by the ancestors of Rinzai Zen to refer to the free human being without vain imaginings, and adds that this alone is incomplete because it leaves unexpressed the "true person that has position." In the following pages of translations from *Shōbōgenzō,* the subtle interweaving of emptiness and existence is described in great detail in Dōgen's own words.

The texts from *Shōbōgenzō* presented here have been translated with a view to preserving form as well as content, on the premise that both are functional parts of the original design, which is arresting and demands close attention. Accordingly, passages and phrases which the original text keeps in Chinese, as well as certain technical terms which seem to stand out for emphasis, have been italicized in the English translation. Exceptions to this practice have been made in certain instances, such as in the case of technical terms in common parlance. For convenience, proper names have been rendered in their Japanese pronunciations.

Needless to say, the incommensurability of languages makes translation an affair which is incomplete and imperfect by its very nature. Even modern Japanese translations of *Shōbōgenzō* are pale indeed in comparison with the original. As with any literature of this caliber, there is actually no way to fully appreciate *Shōbōgenzō* except in the original. But insofar as language compromises experience in any event, there is no reason to reject further compromise of language. Similarly, the brief introductions and annotations which have been added to the each of the following essays from *Shōbōgenzō* should be regarded as a compromise between the projected needs of a general contemporary audience and the demands of Zen literature as an instrument with specific functions. They are not intended to be definitive or exhaustive in any sense, but rather to be merely suggestive of some of the potentials of *Shōbōgenzō*.

Notes

1. The following account, based mainly on *Kenzeiki,* is not intended to be an exhaustive or critical account of Dōgen's life, but merely to show how Dōgen's career is basically seen in Zen lore; accordingly, theoretical problems such as whether or not Dōgen really met Eisai and what all his motives were for leaving the Kyoto area will not be dealt with, being in any event of little or no significance to those of Dōgen's writings which are herein presented. The *Kenzeiki* is at times clearly sectarian and hagiographic, but it is a useful compilation of various available sources; the parts presented here are those which basically accord with earlier sources. Ages are given as in the text, which means that they are counted according to the number of new years, not birthdays.

2. A note in the text of *Kenzeiki* says that the available record of this conversation is in the hand of a sixth-generation Sōtō monk.

3. *Eihei Kōroku,* scroll 3.

4. Taishō Shinshū Daizōkyō (hereafter TT), vol. 47, p. 534a.

5. Ibid., vol. 48, p. 130a.

6. From *Fukanzazengi.* "Thinking about that which is not thinking" can read "thinking about who isn't thinking" or "thinking about what doesn't think." The particle after "not thinking" in the original story makes it attributive, and by convention refers to the unexpressed subject modified by the attributive verbal expression; thus it means contemplating the mind source, the technique of "turning the light around and looking back" *(ekō henshō),* which Dōgen states he is recommending in this treatise as the essential art of *zazen.* The story goes on further to point out that the contemplation which is done in *ekō henshō* is not thinking; that is to say, it is not conceptual or discursive thought. Besides the stories quoted in the text following, there are many such pointers to be found in Zen lore, using terms such as "before any traces appear," "before a single thought arises," "before the Buddha appears in the world," "before the universe is differentiated," and so on, to orient the mind in the *ekō henshō* technique.

7. *Shōbōgenzō Zazenshin* (Iwanami edition), vol.1, p. 397.

8. TT, vol. 47, p. 550a.

9. *Ching-te Chuan-teng lu,* scroll 11.
10. Ibid., scroll 21.
11. TT, vol. 46, p. 550a.
12. Ibid., vol. 47, pp. 311c–312a.
13. *Shōbōgenzō Zuimonki,* trans. T. Cleary, *Record of Things Heard from the Treasury of the Eye of the True Teaching* (Boulder, 1980), p. 109.
14. Ibid., p. 105.
15. *Shōbōgenzō Bendōwa,* vol. 1, pp. 65–66.
16. Ibid., p. 57.
17. Cleary, *Record of Things Heard,* pp. 71–72.
18. *Eihei Kōroku,* scroll 2.
19. *Shōbōgenzō Bendōwa,* vol. 1, p. 55.
20. *Eihei Kōroku,* scroll 4.
21. *Mūlamadhyamakakārikā,* saṃskāra parīkṣā, verse 8.
22. *Eihei Kōroku,* scroll 6.
23. T. Cleary, *The Sayings and Doings of Pai Chang* (Los Angeles, 1979), p. 11.

Great Transcendent Wisdom
(Makahannyaharamitsu)

The subject of this essay, *mahāprajñāpāramitā* in Sanskrit, is the general title and essential theme of one of the major groups of Buddhist scriptures, and is one of the most important issues in Buddhism. Sanskrit *mahā,* meaning "great," conveys the notion of universality. *Prajñā,* often translated as "wisdom," might be rendered as *intense knowledge;* it is commonly described as knowledge of the true nature of things, as being "empty" or lacking absolute, independent existence. *Pāramitā* means "reached the other shore" or "reached the ultimate," and connotes transcendence of mundane limitations, the "other shore" referring to liberation of the mind.

Thus "great transcendent wisdom," as we read it here, means transcendence by universal intense knowledge. The *Treatise on Great Transcendent Wisdom,* a classic work on this teaching, says, "All things are subject to causes and conditions, none are independent. . . . All are born from causes and conditions, and because of this they have no intrinsic nature of their own. Because of having no intrinsic nature, they are ultimately empty. Not clinging to them because they are ultimately empty is called transcendent wisdom."

From this it can be seen that knowledge of "emptiness" is knowledge of conditionality: emptiness, being the absence of independence or own being of conditional things, is not apart from the conditional. This includes all things, whether concrete or abstract, even the items of the Buddhist teachings. Hence transcendent wisdom is that whereby the world, including even the doctrines and means of Buddhism, is transcended, so that there is no clinging to anything. According to Buddhist philosophy, clinging is a prime source of delusion, whether that clinging be to "profane" or "sacred" things. Therefore realization of the relativity, or nonabsoluteness, of all things is at the core of freedom and enlightenment as proposed by Mahayana Buddhism.

However, if it is because of relativity, or conditionality, that all things are "empty," it is equally true that by the very same conditionality they do exist dependently. The tendency to misinterpret "emptiness" nihilistically, whether by intellectual misunderstanding or by mistaking concentration states for insight, is well known and often mentioned in Buddhist texts, especially texts of the Zen schools, where, perhaps due in part to overemphasis on concentration, it seems to have been a not uncommon problem. A thorough reading of Dōgen's *Shōbōgenzō* will reveal that correcting or preventing the tendency toward nihilistic interpretation of emptiness is a major concern of Dōgen's teaching. In this essay, Dōgen identifies phenomena themselves with transcendent wisdom, emphasizing that within so-called nothing or emptiness all things are found, including the facilities, or means, of the Buddhist teachings.

The image Dōgen uses for the realization of wisdom is that of space. As Dōgen says, "Learning wisdom is space, space is learning wisdom." As a common Zen metaphor for the open mind, space may be said to contain all things without being affected by them. The spacelike mind thus is to be distinguished from the mind which is, as it were, *in* space, the former being the nongrasping, nonrejecting openness traditionally preached by Zen, the latter being a concentration state, often practiced by those who seek tranquility and detachment alone. Dōgen here presents the "middle way" in which the emptiness and existence of all things are simultaneously realized, the centerpoint, the balance, of Mahayana Buddhism.

Much of the essay consists of extracts from Buddhist scripture, and a number of technical terms are brought up. It is not imperative to know exactly what these terms refer to in order to understand the essence of the message, for they refer to Buddhist doctrines, practices, and descriptions as part of the totality of phenomena which all exist yet are empty, are empty yet exist. For the sake of convenience, definitions are provided in a glossary appended to the essay.

Great Transcendent Wisdom

The time when the Independent Seer practices profound transcendent wisdom is the whole body's clear vision that the five clusters are all empty. The five clusters are physical form, sensations, perceptions, conditionings, and consciousness. They are five layers of wisdom. *Clear vision* is wisdom.

In expounding and manifesting this fundamental message, we would say form is empty, emptiness is form, form is form, emptiness is empty. It is *the hundred grasses,* it is myriad forms.

Twelve layers of wisdom are the twelve sense-media. There is also eighteen-layer wisdom—eye, ear, nose, tongue, body, intellect, form, sound, smell, taste, touch, phenomena, as well as the consciousness of the eye, ear, nose, tongue, body, and intellect. There is also four layered wisdom, which is suffering, its accumulation, its extinction, and the path to its extinction. Also there is six-layered wisdom, which is charity, morality, forbearance, vigor, meditation, and wisdom. There is also one-layer wisdom, which is manifest in the immediate present, which is unexcelled complete perfect enlightenment. There are also three layers of wisdom, which are past, present, and future. There are also six layers of wisdom, which are earth, water, fire, air, space, and consciousness. Also, four-layered wisdom is constantly being carried out—it is walking, standing, sitting, and reclining.

In the assembly of Shakyamuni Buddha was a monk who thought to himself, "I should pay obeisance to most profound transcendent wisdom. Though there is no origination or extinction of phenomena herein, yet there are available facilities of bodies of precepts, meditation, wisdom, liberation, and knowledge and insight of liberation. Also there are available facilities of the fruit of the stream-enterer, the fruit of the once-returner, the fruit of the nonreturner, and the fruit of the saint. Also there are available facilities of self-enlightenment and enlightening beings. Also there is the available facility of unexcelled true enlightenment. Also there are the available facilities of the Buddha, Teaching, and Community. Also there are the available facilities of the turning of the wheel of the sublime teaching and liberating living beings." The Buddha, knowing what he was thinking, said to the monk, "It is so, it is so. Most profound transcendent wisdom is extremely subtle and hard to fathom."

As for the present monk's *thinking to himself,* where all phenomena are respected, wisdom which still *has no origination or extinction* is *paying obeisance.* Precisely at the time of their obeisance, accordingly wisdom with *available facilities* has become manifest: that is what is referred to as precepts, meditation, wisdom, and so on, up to the liberation of living beings. This is called nothing. The facilities of *nothing* are available in this way. This is transcendent wisdom which is most profound, extremely subtle, and hard to fathom.

> The king of gods asked the honorable Subhūti, "O Great Worthy, if great bodhisattvas want to learn most profound transcendent wisdom, how should they learn it?" Subhūti answered, "If great bodhisattvas want to learn most profound transcendent wisdom, they should learn it like space."

So learning wisdom is space, space is learning wisdom.

> The king of gods also said to the Buddha, "World Honored One, if good men and women accept and hold this most profound transcendent wisdom you have explained, repeat it, reflect upon it in truth, and expound it to others, how should I offer protection?" Then Subhūti said to the king of gods, "Do you see that there is something to protect?" The king said, "No, I do not see that there is anything to protect." Subhūti said, "If good men and women live according to most profound transcendent wisdom as they are taught, that is protection. If good men and women abide in most profound transcendent wisdom as taught here, and never depart from it, no humans or nonhumans can find any way to harm them. If you want to protect the bodhisattvas who live in most profound transcendent wisdom as taught, this is no different from wanting to protect space."

We should know that receiving, holding, repeating, and reflecting reasonably are none other than protecting wisdom. Wanting to protect is receiving and holding and repeating and so on.

My late teacher said, "The whole body is like a mouth hung in space; without question of east, west, south, or north winds, it equally tells others of wisdom. Drop after drop freezes." This is the speaking of wisdom of the lineage of Buddhas and Zen adepts. It is whole body wisdom, whole other wisdom, whole self wisdom, whole east west south north wisdom.

Shakyamuni Buddha said, "Shariputra, living beings should abide in this transcendent wisdom as Buddhas do. They should make offerings, pay obeisance, and contemplate transcendent wisdom just as they make offerings and pay obeisance to the Blessed Buddha. Why? Because transcendent wisdom is not different from the Blessed Buddha, the Blessed Buddha is not different from transcendent wisdom. Transcendent wisdom *is* Buddha, Buddha *is* transcendent wisdom. Why? It is because all those who realize thusness, worthies, truly enlightened ones, appear due to transcendent wisdom. It is because all great bodhisattvas, self-enlightened people, saints, nonreturners, once-returners, stream-enterers, and so on, appear due to transcendent wisdom. It is because all manner of virtuous action in the world, the four meditations, four formless concentrations, and five spiritual powers all appear due to transcendent wisdom."

Therefore the Buddha, the Blessed One, is transcendent wisdom. Transcendent wisdom is all things. These "all things" are the characteristics of emptiness, unoriginated, imperishable, not defiled, not pure, not increasing, not decreasing. The manifestation of this transcendent wisdom is the manifestation of the Buddha. One should inquire into it, investigate it, honor and pay homage to it. This is attending and serving the Buddha, it is the Buddha of attendance and service.

1233

Glossary

Charity, morality, forbearance, vigor, meditation, wisdom: These are the so-called six perfections, or ways of transcendence, one of the basic formulations of Mahayana Buddhism.

Earth, water, fire, air, space, consciousness: These are the "six elements" of which the universe is composed, according to the Shingon school; these elements are said to be the cosmic Buddha itself as well as the substance of all beings, and this is taken as a basic sense in which Buddha and sentient beings are one.

Enlightening beings: This refers to bodhisattvas, people dedicated to enlightenment for all.

Five clusters: According to the Buddhist description, these are basic components, or classes of components, of the body-mind.

Stream-enterer, once-returner, nonreturner, saint: These are four stages of fruition of the way to nirvana—a stream-enterer is one who has begun to be disentangled from the world; a once-returner is one who comes back to the mundane once before attaining release; a nonreturner never comes back; a saint is one who has reached nirvana and is individually emancipated.

Suffering, accumulation, extinction, path to extinction: These are the "four noble truths," or four main axioms, of pristine Buddhism—there is suffering, suffering has a cause, there is an end to suffering, and there is a way to end suffering.

Twelve sense media: This refers to the sense faculties (eye, ear, nose, tongue, body, and mind) and their respective fields of data (form/color, sound, odor, flavor, tactile feelings, and phenomena).

The Issue at Hand
(Genjōkōan)

The term *genjōkōan* seems to appear first in ninth-century China and is often used in Japanese Sōtō Zen to refer to present being as the topic of meditation or the issue of Zen. *Gen* means "manifestation" or "present," *jō* means "become." *Genjō* means actuality—being as is, at hand, or accomplished, as of an accomplished fact. *Kōan* is a common Zen word which is often left untranslated, having to some extent become a naturalized English word. *Kō* means official, public, or open, as opposed to private or personal; *an* means a consideration, or a considered decision. A *kōan* in standard literary Chinese means an official report or an issue under consideration. The term was adopted in Zen with much the same meanings, only transposed into the frame of reference of Zen tradition and experience.

Genjōkōan is one of the most popular and oft-quoted essays in *Shōbōgenzō*. Written to a lay disciple, it contains a number of key points stated in a most concise fashion. The very first paragraph contains a complete outline of Zen, in a covert presentation of the so-called "five ranks" *(go i)* device of the original Chinese Sōtō Zen school. The scheme of the five ranks—relative within absolute, absolute within relative, coming from within the absolute, arriving in the relative, and simultaneous attainment in both relative and absolute—is not overtly used in Dōgen's work, perhaps because of the confusion surrounding it, but its structures are to be found throughout *Shōbōgenzō*.

Following this summary introduction, the essay proceeds to the discussion of enlightenment. Dōgen says the way to enlightenment is to forget the self. The self in this sense refers to an accumulation of habits, including the habit of attachment to this accumulation as a genuine personality. Dōgen calls this forgetting "shedding body and mind," an expression which is said to have galvanized his awareness as a young man and which he repeatedly uses to describe Zen study. Commentators on Dōgen's lectures describe it in these terms: "Each moment of time is thoughtless; things do not provoke a second thought," and "This is the time when the whole mind and body attains great freedom."

This, however, is not the whole issue. In one of his lectures Dōgen says that "shedding body and mind" is the beginning of the effort, and in *Genjōkōan* he affirms that there is continuing progress in buddhahood, going beyond the attainment of enlightenment: "There is ceasing the traces of enlightenment, which causes one to forever leave the traces of enlightenment which is cessation." In the *Hokke* scripture Buddha reveals to his liberated disciples that nirvana, cessation of afflictive habits, which had been expediently represented as the goal, is as it were a resting place on an infinite path.

In the essay *The Business of Progress (or transcendence) of Buddha,* also in *Shōbōgenzō,* Dōgen wrote, "To go on informing the Buddha of today it is not only today is called the business of progress of Buddha." The celebrated Zen master Hakuin said, "Without cultivation and practice after enlightenment, many who have seen the essence miss the boat"; and Hakuin's assistant Tōrei said, "Lesser enlightenment turns out to be a hindrance to great enlightenment. If you give up lesser enlightenments and don't cling to them, great enlightenment will surely be realized." Dōgen says that there are differences in depth and breadth of the realization of enlightenment, and speaks here of enlightenment as being enlightened by all things. This leads to the issue of perspective.

Dōgen states that delusion is a matter of experiencing things with the burden of the self—the bundle of mental habits, ingrained views, which is identified with the self. This is a basic issue of all Buddhist thought. The condition of the self, with its set of conditioned perceptions and views, is implicitly taken as a kind of absolute or veritable point of reference, if one takes one's experience as conceived to be reality. In order to overcome hidden prejudice in the form of unquestioned views, Dōgen says that introspection is necessary, to see that things have no absolute identity, that they are not necessarily or totally as one may view them.

But then Dōgen goes on to point out the absoluteness, so to speak, of relative identity. Logically, if particular things exist, or are defined, relative to one another and therefore lack absolute identity, yet that absolute identitylessness still depends on their relative identity. The approach Dōgen takes, however, is not that of deduction but of direct witness *(genryō),* which he refers to, in classic Zen terminology, as the realms of before and after being disconnected. Thus Dōgen explains the traditional "characteristics of emptiness" called birthlessness and nonperishing in terms of the noncoexistence of before and after, or the nonconcurrence of a state with its own nonexistence. Dōgen's emphasis here seems to be not on discursive understanding of this point of logic, but on presence of mind in the most thoroughgoing sense, direct experience of the present.

Dōgen also speaks of enlightenment in terms of the universal being reflected in the individual; this "merging" of universe and individual does not, however, obliterate the individual or restrict the universal. This leads to the apparent paradox of life being at once finite and infinite. One life, or one sphere of experience, contains everything that is within its scope and nothing that is beyond its range. At every moment we reach, or are at, the full extent of our experience; and yet this never limits the potential of experience in itself. Each moment is complete, hence infinite, in itself, though it be finite as a point of comparison with past or future. In the Kegon philosophy, this interpenetration of the finite and the infinite is represented by the figure of "arriving in one step," each moment of awareness being the focal point of the whole nexus of existence. Again Dōgen drives at the full experience of the present without conceptually delineating it.

Finally Dōgen quotes a classic Zen story alluding to the necessity of practical application even though truth, or enlightenment, is inherent in everyone. A monk asks his teacher why he uses a fan if the nature of wind is eternal and omnipresent; the teacher replies that the student knows the nature of eternity but not the principle of omnipresence, and to illustrate this principle the teacher just fans himself. As one of the Kegon philosophers said, "If not for practice flowing from reality, there is no means to merge with reality."

The Issue at Hand

When all things are Buddha-teachings, then there is delusion and enlightenment, there is cultivation of practice, there is birth, there is death, there are Buddhas, there are sentient beings. When myriad things are all not self, there is no delusion, no enlightenment, no Buddhas, no sentient beings, no birth, no death. Because the Buddha Way originally sprang forth from abundance and paucity, there is birth and death, delusion and enlightenment, sentient beings and Buddhas. Moreover, though this is so, flowers fall when we cling to them, and weeds only grow when we dislike them.

Acting on and witnessing myriad things with the burden of oneself is "delusion." Acting on and witnessing oneself in the advent of myriad things is enlightenment. Great enlightenment about delusion is Buddhas; great delusion about enlightenment is sentient beings. There are also those who attain enlightenment on top of enlightenment, and there are those who are further deluded in the midst of delusion. When the Buddhas are indeed the Buddhas, there is no need to be self-conscious of being Buddhas; nevertheless it is realizing buddhahood—Buddhas go on realizing.

In seeing forms with the whole body-mind, hearing sound with the whole body-mind, though one intimately understands, it isn't like reflecting images in a mirror, it's not like water and the moon—when you witness one side, one side is obscure.

Studying the Buddha Way is studying oneself. Studying oneself is forgetting oneself. Forgetting oneself is being enlightened by all things. Being enlightened by all things is causing the body-mind of oneself and the body-mind of others to be shed. There is ceasing the traces of enlightenment, which causes one to forever leave the traces of enlightenment which is cessation.

When people first seek the Teaching, they are far from the bounds of the Teaching. Once the Teaching is properly conveyed in oneself, already one is the original human being.

When someone rides in a boat, as he looks at the shore he has the illusion that the shore is moving. When he looks at the boat under him, he realizes the boat is moving. In the same way, when one takes things for granted with confused ideas of body-mind, one has the illusion that one's own mind and own nature are permanent; but if one pays close attention to one's own actions, the truth that things are not self will be clear.

Kindling becomes ash, and cannot become kindling again. However, we should not see the ash as after and the kindling as before. Know that kindling abides in the normative state of kindling, and though it has a before and after, the realms of before and after are disconnected. Ash, in the normative state of ash, has before and after. Just as that kindling, after having become ash, does not again become kindling, so after dying a person does not become alive again. This being the case, not saying that life becomes death is an established custom in Buddhism—therefore it is called *unborn*. That death does not become life is an established teaching of the Buddha; therefore we say *imperishable*. Life is an individual temporal state, death is an individual temporal state. It is like winter and spring—we don't think winter becomes spring, we don't say spring becomes summer.

People's attaining enlightenment is like the moon reflected in water. The moon does not get wet, the water isn't broken. Though it is a vast expansive light, it rests in a little bit of water—even the whole moon, the whole sky, rests in a dewdrop on the grass, rests in even a single droplet of water. That enlightenment does not shatter people is like the moon not piercing the water. People's not obstructing enlightenment is like the drop of dew not obstructing the moon in the sky. The depth is proportionate to the height. As for the length and brevity of time, examining the great and small bodies of water, you should discern the breadth and narrowness of the moon in the sky.

Before one has studied the Teaching fully in body and mind, one feels one is already sufficient in the Teaching. If the body and mind are replete with the Teaching, in one respect one senses insufficiency. For example, when one rides a boat out onto the ocean where there are no mountains and looks around, it only appears round, and one can see no other, different characteristics. However, this ocean is not round, nor is it square—the remaining qualities of the ocean are inexhaustible. It is like a palace, it is like ornaments, yet as far as our eyes can see, it only seems round. It is the same with all things—in the realms of matter, beyond conceptualization, they include many aspects, but we see and comprehend only what the power of our eye of contemplative study reaches. If we inquire into the "family ways" of myriad things, the qualities of seas and mountains, beyond seeming square or round, are endlessly numerous. We should realize there exist worlds everywhere. It's not only thus in out of the way places—know that even a single drop right before us is also thus.

As a fish travels through water, there is no bound to the water no matter how far it goes; as a bird flies through the sky, there's no bound to the sky no matter how far it flies. While this is so, the fish and birds have never been apart from the water and the sky—it's just that when the need is large the use is large, and when the requirement is small the use is small. In this way, though the bounds are unfailingly reached everywhere and tread upon in every single place, the bird would instantly die if it left the sky and the fish would instantly die if it left the water. Obviously, water is life; obviously the sky is life. There is bird being life. There is fish being life. There is life being bird, there is life being fish. There must be progress beyond this—there is cultivation and realization, the existence of the living one being like this. Under these circumstances, if there were birds or fish who attempted to traverse the waters or the sky after having found the limits of the water or sky, they wouldn't find a path in the water or the sky—they won't find any place. When one finds this place, this action accordingly manifests as the issue at hand; when one finds this path, this action accordingly manifests as the issue at hand. This path, this place, is not big or small, not self or other, not preexistent, not now appearing—therefore it exists in this way. In this way, if someone cultivates and realizes the Buddha Way, it is *attaining a principle, mastering the principle;* it is *encountering a practice, cultivating the practice.* In this there is a place where the path has been accomplished, hence the unknowability of the known boundary is born together and studies along with the thorough investigation of the Buddha Teaching of this knowing—therefore it is thus. Don't get the idea that the attainment necessarily becomes one's own knowledge and view, that it would be known by discursive knowledge. Though realizational comprehension already takes place, implicit being is not necessarily obvious—*why necessarily* is there obvious becoming?

Zen Master Hōtetsu of Mt. Mayoku was using a fan. A monk asked him about this: "The nature of wind is eternal and all-pervasive —why then do you use a fan?" The master said, "You only know the nature of wind is eternal, but do not yet know the principle of its omnipresence." The monk asked, "What is the principle of its omnipresence?" The master just fanned. The monk bowed.

The experience of the Buddha Teaching, the living road of right transmission, is like this. To say that since (the nature of wind) is permanent one should not use a fan, and that one should feel the breeze even when not using a fan, is not knowing permanence and not knowing the nature of the wind either. Because the nature of wind is eternal, the wind of Buddhism causes the manifestation of the earth's being gold and by participation develops the long river into butter.

1233

The Nature of Things
(Hosshō)

The *nature of things* is a fundamental term of Mahayana Buddhism. It is defined as being the nature of *thusness, emptiness,* and *nirvana.* In pristine Buddhism, nirvana, or "extinction," refers to the attainment of dispassion, peace of mind, freedom from anxiety and mental afflictions. In Mahayana Buddhism, nirvana is commonly used in reference to things, with the meaning of "emptiness." In terms of the person, nirvana refers to the extinction of false description, of fixed views; this results in awareness of the "empty" or "open" nature of things. Emptiness means that things in themselves are indefinable; being dependent on relations, things are said to have no individual or absolute nature of their own. It is this nonabsoluteness which is called emptiness. Another way of expressing it is in terms of inconceivability. The descriptions by which things are defined, and even the experience of things, depend on the mind, and are not the supposed things in themselves. Thus the nature of things in themselves is said to be inconceivable, beyond description, or "empty."

Yet this "emptiness" has no existence of its own either, since it is nothing but the nature of things as relative and identityless. That is to say, the emptiness of things and the relative existence of things are not antithetical but identical in essence. The term *thusness* embraces both of these aspects of reality—the relative existence of things and the emptiness of absolute existence of particular things. These two perspectives are referred to as two facets of thusness—that which is unchanging (absolute emptiness) and that which accords with conditions (relative existence). The term *thusness* itself alludes to the simultaneous realization of emptiness and existence, experiencing directly and openly without fixed conceptual glosses, seeing everything as being simply "thus."

This essay by Dōgen clearly aims at countering the mistaken notion that the nature of things *qua* emptiness is opposed to or exclusive of the appearances of things, or relative existence. This erroneous notion posits the obliteration of appearances as the means of realizing the nature of things, something which Dōgen opposes throughout his works.

Rather than trying to obliterate anything, Dōgen aims at breaking through the barrier of conception to realize the nature of things in everything, to realize the nature of things *is* everything.

The Nature of Things

In meditation study, whether following scripture or following a teacher, one *becomes enlightened alone without a teacher.* Becoming *enlightened alone without a teacher* is the activity of the nature of things. Even though one be *born knowing,* one should seek a teacher to inquire about the Path. Even in the case of *knowledge of the birthless*[1] one should definitely direct effort to mastering the Path. Which individuals are not *born knowing?* Even up to enlightenment, the fruit of buddhahood, it is a matter of following scriptures and teachers. Know that encountering a scripture or a teacher and attaining *absorption in the nature of things* is called the *born knowing* that attains *absorption in the nature of things* on encountering *absorption in the nature of things.* This is attaining knowledge of past lives, attaining the three superknowledges,[2] realizing unexcelled enlightenment, encountering inborn knowledge and learning inborn knowledge, encountering teacherless knowledge and spontaneous knowledge and correctly conveying teacherless knowledge and spontaneous knowledge.

If one were not *born knowing,* even though might encounter scriptures and teachers one could not hear of the *nature of things,* one could not witness the *nature of things.* The *Great Path* is not the principle of *like someone drinking water knows for himself whether it's warm or cool.* All Buddhas as well as all bodhisattvas and all living beings clarify the Great Path of the nature of all things by the power of inborn knowledge. To clarify the *Great Path* of the *nature of things* following scriptures or teachers is called clarifying the *nature of things* by oneself. Scriptures are the nature of things, are oneself. Teachers are the *nature of things,* are oneself. The *nature of things* is the teacher, the *nature of things* is oneself. Because the *nature of things* is oneself, it is not the self misconceived by heretics and demons. In the *nature of things* there are no heretics or demons—it is only *eating breakfast, eating lunch, having a snack.* Even so, those who claim to have studied for a long time, for twenty or thirty years, pass their whole life in a daze when they read or hear talk of the *nature of things.* Those who claim to have fulfilled Zen study and assume the rank of teacher, while they hear the voice of the *nature of things* and see the forms of the *nature of things,* yet their body and mind, objective and subjective experience, always just rise and fall in the pit of confusion. What this is like is wrongly thinking that the *nature of things* will appear when the whole world we perceive is obliterated, that the *nature of things* is not the present totality of phenomena. The principle of the *nature of things* cannot be like this. This *totality of phenomena* and the *nature of things* are far beyond any question of sameness or difference, beyond talk of distinction or identity. It is not past, present, or future, not annihilation or eternity, not form, sensation, conception, conditioning, or consciousness—therefore it is the *nature of things.*

Zen Master Baso said, "All living beings, for infinite eons, have never left absorption in the nature of things: they are always within absorption in the nature of things, wearing clothes, eating, conversing —the functions of the six sense organs, and all activities, all are the nature of things."

The *nature of things* spoken of by Baso is the *nature of things* spoken of by the *nature of things.* It learns from the same source as Baso, is a fellow student of the *nature of things:* since hearing of it takes place, how could there not be speaking of it? The fact is that *the nature of things rides Baso;* it is *people eat food, food eats people.* Ever since the *nature of things,* it has never left *absorption in the nature of things.* It doesn't leave the *nature of things* after the *nature of things,* it doesn't leave the *nature of things* before the *nature of things.* The *nature of things,* along with *infinite eons,* is *absorption in the nature of things;* the *nature of things* is called *infinite eons.* Therefore the *here* of the immediate present is the *nature of things;* the *nature of things* is the *here* of the immediate present. *Wearing clothes and eating food* is the *wearing clothes and eating food of absorption in the nature of things.* It is the manifestation of the *nature of things* of food, it is the manifestation of the *nature of things* of eating, it is the manifestation of the *nature of things* of clothing, it is the manifestation of the *nature of things* of wearing.[3] If one does not dress or eat, does not talk or answer, does not use the senses, does not act at all, it is not the *nature of things*, it is *not entering the nature of things*.

The manifestation of the Path of the immediate present was transmitted by the Buddhas, reaching Shakyamuni Buddha; correctly conveyed by the Zen adepts, it reached Baso. Buddha to Buddha, adept to adept, correctly conveyed and handed on, it has been correctly communicated in *absorption in the nature of things*. Buddhas and Zen adepts, *not entering*, enliven the *nature of things*.[4] Though externalist scholars may have the term *nature of things*, it is not the *nature of things* spoken of by Baso. Though the power to propose that *living beings* who *don't leave the nature of things* are not the *nature of things* may achieve something, this is three or four new layers of the *nature of things*. To speak, reply, function, and act as if it were not the *nature of things* must be the *nature of things*. The days and months of *infinite eons* are the passage of the *nature of things*. The same is so of past, present, and future. If you take the limit of body and mind as the limit of body and mind and think it is far from the *nature of things*, this thinking still is the *nature of things*. If you don't consider the limit of body and mind as the limit of body and mind and think it is not the *nature of things*, this thought too is the *nature of things*. Thinking and not thinking are both the *nature of things*. To learn that since we have said *nature* (it means that) water must not flow and trees must not bloom and wither, is heretical.

Shakyamuni Buddha said, "Such characteristics, such nature." So *flowers blooming* and *leaves falling* are *such nature*. Yet ignorant people think that there could not be *flowers blooming and leaves falling* in the realm of the *nature of things*. For the time being one should not question another. You should model your doubt on verbal expression. Bringing it up as others have said it, you should investigate it over and over again—there will be escape from before.[5] The aforementioned thoughts are not wrong thinking, they are just thoughts while not yet having understood. It is not that this thinking will be caused to disappear when one understands. Flowers blooming and leaves falling are of themselves flowers blooming and leaves falling. The thinking that is thought that there can't be flowers blooming or leaves falling in the *nature of things* is the *nature of things*. It is thought which has fallen out according to a pattern; therefore it is thought of the *nature of things*. The whole thinking of thinking of the *nature of things* is such an appearance.

Although Baso's statement *all is the nature of things* is truly an *eighty or ninety percent* statement, there are many points which Baso has not expressed. That is to say, he doesn't say *the natures of all things do not leave the nature of things,*[6] he doesn't say *the natures of all things are all the nature of things.*[6] He doesn't say *all living beings do not leave living beings,*[7] he doesn't say *all living beings are a little bit of the nature of things,* he doesn't say *all living beings are a little bit of all living beings,*[8] he doesn't say *the natures of all things are a little bit of living beings.*[9] He doesn't say *half a living being is half the nature of things.*[10] He doesn't say *nonexistence of living beings is the nature of things,*[11] he doesn't say *the nature of things is not living beings,*[11] he doesn't say *the nature of things exudes the nature of things,* he doesn't say *living beings shed living beings.* We only hear that living beings do not leave absorption in the nature of things—he doesn't say that the nature of things cannot leave absorption in living beings, there is no statement of absorption in the nature of things exiting and entering absorption in living beings. Needless to say, we don't hear of the attainment of buddhahood of the *nature of things,* we don't hear *living beings realize the nature of things,* we don't hear *the nature of things* realizes the nature of things, there is no statement of how *inanimate beings don't leave the nature of things.* Now one should ask Baso, what do you call "living beings"? If you call the *nature of things* living beings, it is *what thing comes thus?* If you call living beings living beings, it is *if you speak of it as something, you miss it.* Speak quickly, speak quickly!

1243

Notes

1. "The birthless" means emptiness, also immediate experience without comparison of before and after. This line could read "Even if one be without inborn knowledge . . . ," but in Buddhism the term conventionally refers to knowledge of the uncreated.

2. The three superknowledges are paranormal perceptions of saints and Buddhas: knowledge of the features of birth and death of beings in the past, knowledge of the features of birth and death of beings in the future, and knowledge of extinguishing mental contaminations. In Zen all three are sometimes interpreted in reference to insight into the fundamental mind, which is in essence the same in all times and has no inherent contamination.

3. Var. lect. "Clothing is the manifestation of the nature of things, food is the manifestation of the nature of things, eating is the manifestation of the nature of things, wearing is the manifestation of the nature of things."

4. Here "not entering" means that the nature of things is not something external to be entered; rather it is something omnipresent to be lived.

5. This passage seems to point to *kōan* practice, specifically the use of *kosoku kōan* or ancient model *kōan,* Zen sayings or stories used to focus awareness in certain ways. "There will be escape from before" refers to the shedding of former views or states of mind.

6. The (individual) natures of things are not apart from the (universal) nature of things, because individual natures are relative, hence empty of absolute identity—this emptiness itself is the universal nature of things.

7. Living beings *qua* living beings—that is, in terms of relative identity or conditional existence—are always such, by definition.

8. "All living beings" as seen from one point of view (such as that of human perception) are a small part of "all living beings" as seen or experienced from all possible points of reference. This is reminiscent of the Kegon teaching of the infinite interreflection of interdependent existences, and the Tendai teaching of all realms of being mutually containing one another. According to the Tendai doctrine, the totality of living beings is defined in terms of ten realms or universes, but as each contains the potential of all the others, this makes one hundred realms. The Kegon doctrine takes this further and says that each of the latent or potential realms in each realm also contains the latent potential of every other realm, so they are, in terms of their endless interrelation, multiplied and remultiplied infinitely.

9. In terms of the doctrine of the interdependence of everything in the cosmos, as exemplified by the Kegon teaching, all things are a part of the existence of each and every thing and being.

10. Essence (emptiness of absolute identity) and characteristics (existence of relative identity) may be likened to two "halves" of the totality of all existence and the nature of things.

11. "Nonexistence of living beings" as emptiness of an absolute nature of "living beings" is the nature of things *qua* emptiness.

The Whole Works
(Zenki)

This essay is strongly reminiscent of the central teaching of the philosophy of the Kegon school: interdependent origination, and its corollaries dealing with the interpenetration of existence and emptiness, unity and multiplicity.

The word *zenki* consists of two elements: *zen* means "whole" or total or complete; *ki* has many meanings, those relevant to this case including "works" in the sense of machinery, potential, impetus, pivot or vital point, and the flux of nature. *Ki* therefore refers to phenomena in respect to their dynamic aspect, and to the dynamic or vital point itself which underlies, and is revealed by, the active coexistence of phenomena. In Kegon terms, *ki* includes both senses of phenomena and principle, phenomena being interdependent things, the principle being that of interdependence itself. *Zen* refers to the inclusiveness and pervasiveness of *ki* in both senses. We translate *zenki* as "the whole works" to convey by the colloquial sense of this expression the notion of inclusion of the totality of existence, and by the standard sense the notion of the total dynamic underlying the manifestations of existence.

In the Zen classic *Blue Cliff Record*, the sixty-first case says, "If a single atom is set up, the nation flourishes; if a single atom is not set up, the nation perishes." This essay of Dōgen's may be said to center around a restatement of this theme: "In life the whole works is manifest; in death the whole works is manifest," or, to render the same passage another way, "Life is the manifestation of the whole works; death too is the manifestation of the whole works."

In terms of the existence-emptiness equation, from the point of view of existence (represented by the terms "set up" and "life") all that is exists, while from the point of view of emptiness ("not set up," "death") all is empty. The concurrence of existence and emptiness is not as separate entities, but as different aspects or perspectives on the same totality. To borrow Kegon terms again, life as the manifestation of the whole works illustrates *ki* as phenomena, while death as the manifestation of the whole works illustrates *ki* as noumenon.

The passage from the *Blue Cliff Record* alludes to the Kegon doctrine that phenomena do not exist individually but interdependently, that the manifold depends on the unit and the unit on the manifold. A refinement of this principle in Kegon philosophy is called the mystery of principal and satellites: this means that every element in a conditional nexus can be looked upon as the hub, or "principal," whereupon all the other elements become the cooperative conditions, or "satellites"—hence all elements are at once "principal" and "satellite" to all other elements. It is the mutuality, the complementarity, of the elements which makes them functionally what they are. Dōgen presents this idea by likening life to riding in a boat—one is naught without the boat, yet it is one's riding in it that makes it in effect a "boat." Furthermore, "the boat is the world—even the sky, the water, and the shore are circumstances of the boat. . . . The whole earth and all of space are workings of the boat."

The distinction of existence and emptiness, the noncontradiction and mutual interpenetration of existence and emptiness, and thereby the transcendence of existence and emptiness—these are traditional steps of Mahayana Buddhist dialectic. In this essay they are presented by Dōgen in his subtle, almost covert way, evidently to induce the reader to search out these insights by personal contemplation. The ultimate vision of totality, in which the whole and the individuals foster one another—the crown of Kegon Buddhist metaphysics—is one of the fundamental themes of Dōgen's philosophical writings, to be met with time and again in various guises. In this essay it is conveyed in a most succinct manner, worthy of representing Zen Buddhist philosophy.

The Whole Works

The Great Path of the Buddhas, in its consummation, is passage to freedom, is actualization. That passage to freedom, in one sense, is that life passes through life to freedom, and death too passes through death to freedom. Therefore, there is leaving life and death, there is entering life and death; both are the Great Path of consummation. There is abandoning life and death, there is crossing over life and death; both are the Great Path of consummation.

Actualization is life, life is actualization. When that actualization is taking place, it is without exception the complete actualization of life, it is the complete actualization of death. This pivotal working can cause life and cause death. At the precise moment of the actualization of this working, it is not necessarily great, not necessarily small, not all-pervasive, not limited, not extensive, not brief.

The present life is in this working, this working is in the present life. Life is not coming, not going, not present, not becoming. Nevertheless, life is the manifestation of the whole works, death is the manifestation of the whole works. Know that among the infinite things in oneself, there is life and there is death. One should calmly think: is this present life, along with the myriad things concomitant with life, together with life or not? There is nothing at all, not so much as one time or one phenomenon, that is not together with life. Even be it a single thing, a single mind, none is not together with life.

Life is like when one rides in a boat: though in this boat one works the sail, the rudder, and the pole, the boat carries one, and one is naught without the boat. Riding in the boat, one even causes the boat to be a boat. One should meditate on this precise point. At this very moment, the boat is the world—even the sky, the water, and the shore all have become circumstances of the boat, unlike circumstances which are not the boat. For this reason life is our causing to live; it is life's causing us to be ourselves. When riding in a boat, the mind and body, object and subject, are all workings of the boat; the whole earth and all of space are both workings of the boat. We that are life, life that is we, are the same way.

Zen Master Engo Kokugon said, "In life the whole works appears; in death the whole works appears." One should thoroughly investigate and understand this saying. What thorough investigation means is that the principle of *in life the whole works appears* has nothing to do with beginning and end; though it is the whole earth and all space, not only does it not block *the appearance of the whole works in life,* it doesn't block *the appearance of the whole works in death* either. When *the whole works appears in death,* though it is the whole earth and all space, not only does it not block *the appearance of the whole works in death,* it doesn't block *the appearance of the whole works in life* either. For this reason, life doesn't obstruct death, death doesn't obstruct life. The whole earth and all space are in life and in death too. However, it is not fulfilling the potential of one whole earth and one whole space in life and fulfilling their potential in death too. Though they are not one, they are not different; though they are not different, they are not identical; though they are not identical, they are not multiple. Therefore, in life there are myriad phenomena of the appearance of the whole works, and in death too there are myriad phenomena of the appearance of the whole works. There is also the manifestation of the whole works in what is neither life nor death.

In the manifestation of the whole works there is life and there is death. Therefore, the whole works of life and death must be like a man bending and straightening his arm. Herein there are so many spiritual powers and lights which are manifest. At the moment of manifestation, because it is completely activated by manifestation, one sees and understands that there is no manifestation before manifestation. However, prior to this manifestation is previous manifestation of the whole works. Although there is previous manifestation of the whole works, it is does not block the present manifestation of the whole works. For this reason, such a vision and understanding vigorously appears.

1242

Such
(Immo)

This essay begins with a saying of an ancient master: "To attain such a thing, you must be such a person; since you are such a person, why trouble about such a thing?" This is an extract from a longer speech describing the Zen adept, in the course of which the master said, "One who has comprehended has a mind like a fan in winter, has a mouth growing moldy (from disuse). This is not something you force—it is naturally so. If you want to attain such a thing, you must be such a person. Since (or, Once) you are such a person, why trouble about such a thing?"

The word used here for "such," *immo* in Sino-Japanese, is a colloquial word which is equivalent to a classical word used in Buddhism for the term *thusness,* being-as-is, the all-inclusive reality. A lesson that might be drawn from this saying is that thusness, or *suchness,* is arrived at by merging with it; it is not something obtained externally —since you are *thus,* or once you realize you are *thus,* why worry about *thusness* as something to attain? This is basic Zen teaching. That which obstructs the consciousness from realizing oneness with *thusness* is arbitrary conception and false description projected by the mind; hence the saying that one who comprehends has a mind (unused) like a fan in winter and a mouth growing mold (from disuse) might be interpreted as meaning realization of thusness is a matter of not obscuring it by mental construction and fixed labels. Cessation of compulsive mental habits and silencing of the mind are a means of accomplishing this.

Dōgen returns to this theme of being *such* or *thus* throughout the essay. He illustrates the fundamental and all-embracing nature of *suchness* by the traditional saying "If one falls on the ground, one must rise from the ground." Understanding suchness as the "ground" of being leads to the insight that both illusion and enlightenment are based on this ground and have no existence apart from it. In characteristic fashion, Dōgen proceeds to vary this statement, now using the metaphor of "sky" for emptiness and "ground" for existence, to illustrate the countering of one-sided clinging.

Subsequently Dōgen brings up two stories from the lore of the Zen
patriarchs which appear to say that the events of the environment are
objectifications of mind. This is a familiar Buddhist concept, but here
Dōgen aims at doing away with the misinterpretation that the world
of sense exists because of mind or is in the mind. What Dōgen indi-
cates is that, to use a classic statement, while things are empty in themselves, yet they exist inconceivably; the product of the mind is not
things in themselves but the subjective description. It is this description which separates subject and object and interferes with pure
awareness of being as *such*. The essay concludes with two Zen stories
illustrating the inapplicability of concepts—even that of "suchness"—
to *suchness* as it really is, and two aspects of Zen "method"—nongrasping and observation without conceptualization.

Such

Master Ungo was the heir of Tōzan, a thirty-ninth generation religious descendant of Shakyamuni Buddha, and a principal ancestor of the Tōzan school. One day he said to the congregation, "If you want to attain such a thing, you must be such a person. Since you are such a person, why trouble about such a thing?" That is to say, to consider attaining *such a thing,* one must be *such a person;* already being *such a person,* why trouble about *such a thing?* The basic message of this is *directly proceeding toward unexcelled enlightenment* is for the moment called *such.* As for what this unexcelled enlightenment is like, even *all worlds in the ten directions* are a little bit of unexcelled enlightenment; the extent of enlightenment must be even more than all worlds. We too are all equipment within those worlds of the ten directions.

Whereby do we know *suchness* exists? It is as if to say body and mind together appear in the whole world, and because they are not self, we know they are *thus.* Since the body is not oneself, life is borne along by the passage of time, hardly to be kept for even a moment. Rosy cheeks have gone away somewhere—as they vanish, there are no traces. When we look carefully, there are many things gone which we can never see again. The red heart doesn't stay either—it comes and goes bit by bit. Though we might say there is truth, it is not something that lingers in the region of ego and self.

There are those who, being *such,* are inspired spontaneously. Once this inspiration occurs, they give up what they had hitherto been fascinated with, hope to learn what they haven't yet learned, and seek to realize what they haven't realized—this is totally not the doing of the self. Know that one is thus because one is *such a person.* How do we know one is *such a person?* We know one is *such a person* because one wants to attain *such a thing.* Since one has the face of *such a person,* one shouldn't trouble about this *such a thing.* Because troubling too is *such a thing,* it is not trouble. Also one should not be surprised at *such a thing's* being *such.* Even if there is *suchness* which seems strange, this too is *such*—there is the *suchness* of "one should not be surprised." This is not to be measured simply by the measure of Buddha, it is not to be measured by the measure of mind, it is not to be measured by the measure of the realm of phenomena and principles, it is not to be measured by the measure of the whole world—it can only be *since you are such a person, why trouble about such a thing?*

Therefore, the *suchness* of sound and form must be *such;* the *suchness* of body and mind must be *such;* the *suchness* of the Buddhas must be *such.* For example, in *understanding as such* the time of *falling on the ground* as being *such,* at the time of the *suchness* of *necessarily rising from the ground,* one does not think *falling on the ground* strange. There is a statement that has been made from antiquity, that has been made from India, that has been made from heaven: *if one falls on the ground, one rises from the ground; there is no way to rise apart from the ground.* What this is saying is that one who falls on the ground must get up from the ground, and cannot hope to rise except by way of the ground. It has been considered excellent to become greatly enlightened when this is brought up, and considered a path to liberate body and mind as well. Therefore, if one asks what the principle of enlightenment of the Buddhas is, it is said to be like someone fallen on the ground rising from the ground. One should investigate this and pass through the past to freedom, should pass through the future to freedom, should pass through the present *suchness* to freedom.

Greatly enlightened, not becoming enlightened, returning to delusion, losing delusion, being blocked by enlightenment, being blocked by delusion are all the principle of one fallen on the ground rising from the ground. This is a saying of heaven and earth, of India and China, of past, present, and future, of ancient Buddhas and new Buddhas. This saying has left nothing unsaid, it has no lack. However, if one only understands *so* and has no understanding of *not so,* it is as though one has not thoroughly investigated this saying.

Even though the saying of the ancient Buddhas has come down

thus, if one would go on to hear the ancient Buddhas' saying as an ancient Buddha, one must have hearing beyond this. Though it hasn't been said in India or in the heavens, there is a further principle to express. That is, if one fallen to the ground tries to arise from the ground, one can never ever rise. In truth, one manages to arise from a *living road.* That is to say, one fallen to the ground must arise from the sky, and one fallen to the sky must arise from the ground. Otherwise one can never get up. All the Buddhas and Zen adepts were thus. If someone were to ask thus: "How far apart are sky and ground?" Thus asked, I would answer thus: sky and ground are one hundred and eight thousand miles apart.[1] *If one falls to the ground, one must arise from the sky; if one tries to arise apart from the sky, there will never be a way. If one falls to the sky one must arise from the ground; if one tries to arise apart from the ground, there will never be a way.* If one has not yet expressed it in this way, one does not yet know, does not yet see the measure of the *ground* and *sky* spoken of by Buddha.

The seventeenth-generation ancestral teacher of Buddhism was the honorable Sanghanandi; his religious successor was Gayashata. Once, hearing the chimes hung in a chamber ring when blown by the wind, he asked Gayashata, "Would you say the wind is ringing or are the chimes ringing?" Gayashata said, "It is not the wind ringing or the chimes ringing; it is my mind ringing." Sanghanandi said, "And what is the mind?" Gayashata said, "Both are silent." Sanghanandi said, "Good, good! Who but you could succeed to my way?" Subsequently he imparted the *treasury of the eye of true teaching* to him.

This is studying *my mind ringing* where it is not wind ringing, and studying *my mind ringing* when it is not chimes ringing. Though *my mind ringing* is *such,* yet *both are silent.* Transmitted from India to China, from ancient times to the present day, this story has been taken as a standard for study of the Way, yet there are many who misunderstand it. It is said that Gayashata's statement that it is not the wind ringing or the chimes ringing, but the mind ringing, means that at such a moment of the hearer thought arises, and this arising of thought is called mind; if this mental thought were not there, how could the mind focus on the sound of ringing—because hearing takes place due to this thought, it should be called the basis of hearing, and so it is called mind. This is a misinterpretation, all due to not having gotten the power of a true teacher. It is like the interpretation of linguistic philosophers.[2] This kind of interpretation is not the mystic study of the Buddha Way.

What one learns from a true heir of the Buddha Way is that the *treasury of the eye of true teaching* of unexcelled enlightenment is called *silent*,[3] is called *uncreated,* is called *samādhi,*[4] is called *dhāraṇī*.[5] The principle is that as soon as one thing is *silent,* myriad things are *silent.* Since the wind blowing is *silent,* the chimes ringing is *silent.* This is why he said *both are silent.* He is saying the *mind ringing* is not the *wind ringing,* the *mind ringing* is not the *chimes ringing,* the *mind ringing* is not the *mind ringing.* If we would closely investigate it as *such,* we should simply say further that it is the wind ringing, it is the chimes ringing, it is the blowing ringing, it is the ringing ringing—we could also say this. Because *why trouble over such a thing,* it is not existing as *such;*[6] since it is *why be concerned with such a thing,* it is *such.*[6]

When the thirty-third ancestor of Buddhism, the sixth patriarch of Zen, was lodging in Hosshō monastery in Canton before his ordination, there were two monks arguing, one saying it is the flag moving, one saying it is the wind moving. As they argued ceaselessly back and forth like this, the patriarch said, "It is not the wind moving, it is not the flag moving—it is your minds moving." The two monks immediately accepted this.

Those two monks had come from India. So in this statement the patriarch says that the wind, the flag, and the movement are all the mind. In fact, though people now hear this statement, they do not know it; much less are they able to express what the patriarch said. Why do I say so? Hearing the saying *your minds are moving,* to say *your minds are moving* while trying to say *your minds are moving* is not to see the patriarch, is not to be a descendant of the teaching of the patriarch. Now as descendants of the patriarch, saying what the patriarch said, saying it with the body and limbs, hair and skin of the patriarch, we should speak thus: be *your minds moving* as it may, we should say *you are moving.* Why do I say so? Because since *that which is moving is moving,* therefore *you are you.* Because of *already being such a person* one *speaks in such a way.* This sixth patriarch of Zen used to be a woodcutter in south China. He knew the mountains and streams thoroughly. Though he worked under the green pines and cut through the roots, how could he know of the existence of ease inside a monastery and of ancient teachings which illumine the mind? From whom did he learn self-discipline and purification? He heard a scripture being recited in the marketplace— this was not something he himself anticipated, nor was it enjoined upon him by another. He lost his father as a boy, and supported his mother when he grew up. He didn't know this jewel in his clothing[7] shone through heaven and earth. Once he was suddenly enlightened, he left his mother and sought a teacher—this is rare behavior among people. For whom are gratitude and love insignificant? He gave up sentiments because he considered the truth more important. This is the principle of how if people with wisdom hear *they can immediately believe and understand.* "Wisdom" is not learned in people, it doesn't arise of itself; wisdom is communicated to wisdom, wisdom seeks wisdom. In the case of the five hundred bats,[8] wisdom spontaneously consumed their bodies and they had no more body or mind. As for the ten thousand floundering fish,[9] wisdom itself was their bodies, so even though it wasn't condition or cause, when they heard the Teaching they immediately understood. It is not a matter of coming or entering. It's like the spirit of spring meeting the spring. Wisdom is not imbued with thought, wisdom is not devoid of thought; wisdom is not mindful, wisdom is not mindless—how much less has it to do with great or small, how much less is it a question of delusion or enlightenment. What we're saying is that (the sixth patriarch of Zen) didn't know anything about Buddhism, and since he hadn't heard about it before, he didn't admire or seek it, yet nevertheless when he heard the teaching, he neglected sentiment and forgot himself, all due to the fact that the body-mind with wisdom is already not oneself. This is called being *immediately able to believe and understand.*

Who knows how many cycles of birth and death we have gone

through in vain sensual toils while having this wisdom. It is like a rock containing a jewel, the jewel not knowing it is enclosed in rock, and the rock not knowing it contains a jewel. People know of it and take it —this is not anticipated or awaited by the jewel or the rock, it doesn't depend on the rock's knowledge or insight, and it is not the thought of the jewel. So it is as if in spite of the fact that the person and wisdom do not know one another, the Way is surely heard by wisdom. There is a saying: *lacking wisdom, doubt and suspicion then is an eternal loss.* Though wisdom is not necessarily existent, and not necessarily nonexistent, there is existence which is one time's *spring pines,* there is nonexistence which is *autumn chrysanthemums.* When there is no wisdom, perfect enlightenment all becomes *doubt and suspicion,* all things are *doubt and suspicion.* At this time *eternal loss then is.* The Way which is to be heard, the principle to be realized, then are *doubt and suspicion.*

The whole world, which is not self, has no hidden place; it is *a single rail of iron ten thousand miles long* which is not anyone. Even if branches sprout *thus,* the fact is that *in the Buddha lands of the ten directions there is only the teaching of one vehicle.* Even if leaves fall *thus,* the fact is that *these phenomena abide in their normal state—the features of the world are permanent.* Because it is already such a thing, having wisdom and not having wisdom are *sun face* and *moon face.*[10]

Because he was *such a person,* the sixth patriarch of Zen too was awakened. Subsequently he went to Mt. Ōbai and paid his respects to the Zen master Daiman, who sent him down to the workers' building. When he had been pounding rice day and night for a mere eight months, one night when it was very late Daiman himself stole into the millery and asked, "Is the rice polished yet?" He said, "It's polished but not sifted." Daiman struck the mortar thrice with his staff, whereupon the sixth patriarch sifted the rice in the sieve thrice. This is called the moment of the meshing of the path of teacher and apprentice. Though one doesn't know oneself and others do not understand, the *transmission of the teaching and the robe* is indeed the *precise time* of being *such.*

Master Sekitō was asked by Yakuzan, "I have a rough knowledge of the canonical teaching of Buddhism, but I've heard that in the South they directly point to the human mind, see its nature, and attain buddhahood—I really do not understand this, and hope you will be so compassionate as to give me some indication of it." This is a question of Yakuzan, who originally was a lecturer. He had mastered the canonical Buddhist teachings, so it seemed there was nothing further about Buddhism that was not clear to him. In ancient times, before the separate schools had arisen, just to understand the canonical teachings was considered the way of doctrinal study. Nowadays many people, being stupid, set up individual schools and assess Buddhism this way, but this is not the rule of the Buddha Way. In reply to Yakuzan's question, Sekitō said, *It cannot be grasped as such, it cannot be grasped as not such—as such or not such, it cannot be grasped at all: what about you?* This is the great master's statement for Yakuzan. Truly, because it *cannot be grasped at all, as such or not such,* therefore *it cannot be grasped as such, it cannot be grasped as not such. Such* means *thus.* It is not limited needs for the way, it is not unlimited needs for the way. *Suchness* should be studied in *nongrasping,* and *nongrasping* should be sought in *suchness.* This *suchness* and *nongrasping* are not only confined to the measure of Buddha. It is *understanding not grasping; it is realizing not grasping.*[11]

The sixth patriarch of Zen said to Zen Master Daie of Nangaku, *What thing comes thus?* This saying is because *thus* is nondoubting, is nonunderstanding. Because it is *what thing is it,* myriad things must be investigated as being *what thing;* one thing must be investigated as being *what thing. What thing* is not doubting—it is *thus come.*

1242

Notes

1. 108,000 stands for all delusions or attachments: "sky" and "earth," or emptiness and existence, are in essence identical, and what stands between them, or what blocks realization of their unity, are subjective delusions or attachments to appearances.

2. Literally "the teachers of 'relying on the principal' and 'association' "— these expressions refer to two kinds of Sanskrit compounds, *avyayībhāva*

(indeclinable) and *tatpuruṣa* (determinative). The latter is described in Chinese as establishing the name of the dependent element based on the depended-upon element; the former is defined as establishing a name based on the dominant associated element.

3. "Silent" means "empty," referring to emptiness of absolute existence.

4. *Samādhi* means mental concentration or absorption, but in Zen literature it is often used loosely to refer to a spiritual state or realization.

5. A *dhāraṇī* is a mystical incantation in which teachings are concentrated; in Zen literature this term is sometimes used loosely to refer to spiritual realization.

6. It doesn't "exist" as such as an external thing to grasp—yet there would be no experience in the case of total nonexistence, so it must be *such*.

7. A metaphor for inherent Buddha-potential, from the *Hokke* scripture. While a traveler is intoxicated, a benefactor sews a priceless jewel in his robe. The traveler, unaware of the jewel, goes to another country and ekes out a living, suffering much hardship. Later he again meets his benefactor, who calls his attention to the jewel in his robe.

8. Five hundred bats were living in a tree. A group of traveling merchants stopped there and their campfire spread to the tree. Even while the tree they lived in burned, the bats did not flee but remained there to listen to one of the people reciting holy writ, and were consumed in the flames. Because of this the bats were reborn as humans and became sages.

9. As ten thousand fish were about to die in a dried up lake, someone gave them food and water and also expounded Buddhism to them. The fish died and were reborn in heaven due to listening to the teaching.

10. Dōgen said, "Truly the Way has no obstruction—rich and poor, high and low, old and young, ignorant and slow, all travel on it. The glorious magnificence of buddhahood comes from the Way, and even evildoers have a part in it." Also, "Birth and death, desire for food and drink and warmth, growing up, anger and joy, gain and loss, going and returning, all are as such because there is one great Way without obstruction." *(Eihei Kōroku)*

11. Using Sung dynasty Chinese grammar, this could be read, "This cannot be understood, cannot be realized."

One Bright Jewel
(Ikka Myōju)

This essay emphasizes the total unity of being, a persistent theme of Dōgen's writings and sayings. It is based on a well-known saying of a famous teacher of ancient times, that the whole world, or all worlds, the whole universe, is "one bright jewel." When a student asked that teacher how to understand this saying, he said, "What's it got to do with understanding?" or "Why do you want to understand?" or "What's the use of understanding?" Each of these points is worth reflecting upon, but an underlying message applying to any way we might read this reply seems to be that the unity of being is so whether or not anyone consciously understands it; being is not made one by means of understanding. Furthermore, conceptual understanding, with its inherent discrimination, can obscure rather than reveal this unity, should one "miss the forest for the trees."

However, this does not mean that the only alternative is ignorance: in the story, when the student hands the teacher back the same answer on the following day, the teacher makes a remark suggesting that the student is clinging to nonunderstanding, or simply hanging on to a slogan in place of true understanding. Throughout this essay Dōgen shows how to avoid missing the whole for the parts while at the same time still appreciating the infinite variety of particulars as "adornments" of the whole, as "lights" of the "one jewel."

One Bright Jewel

The great master Gensha had the religious name Shibi; his lay surname was Sha. In lay life he enjoyed fishing and used to ply his boat on the Nandai river, following the ways of the fishermen. He must have had, *without expectation,* the *golden fish* which *comes up by itself without being fished out.* At the beginning of the Kantsū era of the Tang dynasty (860–873), he suddenly wished to *leave the world;* he left his boat and went into the mountains. He was thirty years old at the time. Realizing the peril of the ephemeral world, he came to know the lofty value of the Buddha Way. Finally he climbed Snowy Peak Mountain, called on the great Zen master Seppō, and worked on the Way day and night.

One time, in order to make a thorough study of Zen as taught all over the country, he took his knapsack and headed out of the mountain, but on the way he stubbed his toe on a rock, and as it bled painfully, he suddenly had a powerful insight and said, *This body is not existent—where does pain come from?* So he then went back to Seppō. Seppō asked him, *Which one is the ascetic Shibi?* Gensha said, *I never dare fool people.* Seppō especially liked this saying, and said, "Who does not have this saying? Who can utter this saying?" Seppō asked further, "Ascetic Shibi, why don't you travel to study?" He replied, *Bodhidharma did not come to China, the second patriarch did not go to India.*[1] Seppō particularly praised him for this saying. Because he had up to then been a fisherman, he had never seen the various scriptures and treatises even in dreams, yet nevertheless because the depth of his aspiration was paramount, a determined spirit beyond others had appeared. Seppō thought him outstanding in the community and praised him as being a standard among his disciples. He dressed in plain muslin, and because he never replaced his one robe, it was all patched. He used paper for his underclothing, and also wore mugwort plants. He didn't call on any teacher except Seppō. Nevertheless, he had accomplished the power to inherit his teacher's way.

After he had finally attained the Way, he said to people, *The whole world in all ten directions is a single bright jewel.* Then a monk asked, *I hear you have a saying, that the whole world in all ten directions is one bright jewel—how can a student understand this?* The master said, *The whole world in all ten directions is one bright jewel—what does it have to do with understanding?* The next day the master asked that monk, *The whole world in all ten directions is one bright jewel— how do you understand?* The monk replied, *The whole world in all ten directions is one bright jewel—what does it have to do with understanding?* The master said, *I knew you were making a living in a ghost cave in the mountain of darkness.*[2]

This saying, the whole world in all ten directions is one bright jewel, began with Gensha. The essential message is that *the whole universe* is not *vast,* not *small,* not *round or square,* not *balanced and correct,* not *lively and active,* not *standing way out.* Because furthermore it is not *birth and death, coming and going,* it is *birth and death, coming and going.* Being thus, *having in the past gone from here,* it *now comes from here.* In making a thorough investigation someone must see through it as being weightless, someone must find out it is being single-minded.

All ten directions is the *nonceasing* of *pursuing things as oneself, pursuing oneself as things.* Expressing *when emotions arise wisdom is blocked* as blockage is *turning the head, changing the face,* it is *setting forth events, meeting the situation.* Because of *pursuing self as things,* it is the *all ten directions* which is *unceasing.* Because it is the principle of incipience, there is superabundance in the mastery of the pivot of function. *Is one bright jewel,* though not yet a name, is expression. This has come to be taken as a name. As for *one bright jewel,* it is *even ten thousand years;* as it *extends through antiquity, yet unfinished,* it *extends through the present, having arrived.* Though there is *the present of the body* and *the present of the mind,* it is *a bright jewel.* It is not the *plants and trees* of *here and there,* not the *mountains and rivers* of *heaven and earth*—it is *a bright jewel.*

How can a student understand? As for this saying, even if it seems that the monk was *sporting active consciousness*, it is *the great function manifesting being a great rule.* Going onward, one should cause *a foot of water, a foot of wave*[3] to stand out high. This is what is called *ten feet of jewel, ten feet of brightness.* To express what he meant to say, Gensha said, *The whole world in all ten directions is one bright jewel—what does it have to do with understanding?* This saying is an expression of Buddhas succeeding to Buddhas, Zen adepts succeeding to Zen adepts, Gensha succeeding to Gensha. In trying to escape succession, though it is not that there could be no place to escape, even if one clearly escapes for the time being, as long as there is the arising of expression, it is the covering of time by manifestation.

The next day Gensha asked that monk, "The whole world in all ten directions is one bright jewel—how do you understand?" This says, *yesterday I spoke a definite principle;* today, using a second layer, he *exudes energy*[4]—*today I speak the indefinite principle*—he is *pushing yesterday over, nodding and laughing.* The monk said, "The whole world in all ten directions is one bright jewel—what does understanding have to do with it?" We could call this *riding a thief's horse in pursuit of the thief.* In an ancient Buddha's explanation for you, it is *acting among different species.*[5] For a time you should *turn the light around and introspect*—how many levels of *what has it to do with understanding* are there? In trying to say, though one may say it is *seven milk pancakes, five vegetable pancakes,* this is the teaching and practice of *south of Shō, north of Tan.*[6]

Gensha said, "I knew you were making a living in a ghost cave in the mountain of darkness." Know that *sun face, moon face*[7] has never changed since remote antiquity. *Sun face* comes out together with *sun face,* and *moon face* comes out together with *moon face,* so therefore *if the sixth month you say is just the right time, you cannot say your nature is mature.*[8] Therefore the beginning or beginninglessness of this *bright jewel* has no point of reference—it is *the whole world in all ten directions is one bright jewel.* He doesn't say two or three—the *whole body* is one single *eye of truth,* the *whole body* is the *embodiment of reality,* the *whole body* is one phrase, the *whole body* is light, the *whole body* is the whole body. When being the *whole body,* the *whole body* has no obstruction—it is *perfectly round, it rolls smoothly.* Because the qualities of the *bright jewel* are thus manifest, there are the *Kannon and Miroku*⁹ of the present *seeing form and hearing sound,* there are the *old Buddhas and new Buddhas* who *appear physically to expound the truth.* At *this precise time,* be it hung in the sky, or inside one's clothing, or under the jaw, or in the topknot, in each case it is *the whole world in all ten directions is one bright jewel.* Hanging it inside the clothing is considered to be the way—don't say you'll hang it on the outside. Hanging it in the topknot or under the jaw is considered to be the way—don't try to sport it on the outside of the topknot or jaw. There is a close friend who gives the jewel to you while you're intoxicated with wine—to a close friend the jewel should be given. At the time when the jewel is hung, one is always intoxicated with wine. *Being thus* is the *one bright jewel* which is *the whole world in the ten directions.* This being so, then though it seems to go changing faces, turning or not turning, yet it is *a bright jewel.* It is precisely knowing that the jewel has all along been thus that is itself the *bright jewel.* The *bright jewel* has *sound and form* which sounds this way. In being *already at thusness,* as far as worrying that oneself is not the *bright jewel* is concerned, one should not suspect that that is not the jewel. Worrying and doubting, grasping and rejection, action and inaction are all but temporary views of small measure. What is more, it is merely causing resemblance to small measure. Isn't it lovely —such lusters and lights of the *bright jewel* are unlimited. Each flicker, each beam, of each luster, each light, is a quality of the whole world in all ten directions. Who can take them away? There is no one casting a tile in the marketplace.¹⁰ Don't bother about *not falling into* or *not being blind to*¹¹ the cause and effect of mundane existences— the unclouded original bright jewel which is *true through and through* is the face; the *bright jewel* is the eyes.

However, for me and you both, the *thinking of everything, not thinking of anything* which doesn't know what is the *bright jewel* and what is not the *bright jewel* may have gathered fodder of clarity, but if we have, by way of Gensha's saying, also heard and known and understood what the body and mind which are the *bright jewel* are like, the mind is not oneself—as being who would we bother to grasp or reject becoming and extinction as being the *bright jewel* or not being the *bright jewel?* Even if we doubt and worry, that does not mean it is not that this is not the *bright jewel.* Since it is not action or thought caused by something existing which is not the *bright jewel,* the simple fact is that *forward steps and backward steps* in the *ghost cave in the mountain of darkness* are just *one bright jewel.*

1238

Notes

1. The implication of this is that reality is omnipresent.

2. "Ghost cave in the mountain of darkness" is usually used in Zen to refer to being sunk in quiescence, stillness, formless concentration, nonknowing. It is also called falling into one-sided emptiness or nihilistic emptiness. This is its usage in reference to meditation; it is also used to refer to clinging to stagnant, stereotyped concepts.

3. "Water" stands for essence, emptiness, noumenon; "waves" stands for characteristics, appearances, phenomena. "A foot of water, a foot of wave" refers to perfect realizational integration of emptiness and existence.

4. "Exude energy" or "show life" is used to refer to active function or flexibility, not being stuck in one position or cliche.

5. "Acting among different species" is a technical term in the Chinese parent school of Sōtō Zen and basically means acting in the world in whatever forms may be appropriate. Sōzan (Ts'ao shan), a progenitor of the school, wrote, "Bodhisattvas' assimilation to different species means first understanding oneself, then after that entering the different kinds in birth and death to save others; having already realized nirvana, they do not abandon creatures in birth and death—helping themselves and others, they vow that all sentient beings shall attain buddhahood." Sōzan discusses various types or aspects of "acting among different species," but in general "different species" means the world of differentiation, all kinds of different forms and states.

6. "Seven milk pancakes, five vegetable pancakes" means "everything," and "south of Shō, north of Tan," means "everywhere" (cf. *Blue Cliff Record,* case 18). Everything is "the bright jewel," everything everywhere is *thusness*—specific understandings or descriptions have their place and use, but are by nature fragmentary and do not capture the whole. Yet since this principle extends to all specifics, as the Kegon philosophy emphasizes, one is all and all are one. In Zen synecdoche, any particular object can be used to represent all being.

7. Cf. *Blue Cliff Record,* case 3.

8. An ancient teacher said, "Every day is a good day." Cf. *Blue Cliff Record,* case 6.

9. Kannon is Avalokiteśvara, the bodhisattva of compassion; Miroku is Maitreya, the bodhisattva of kindness.

10. "Casting a tile" to draw a piece of jade means to give a little to get more; someone once posted two lines of verse in a temple where a famous poet was expected to visit, provoking the poet to complete the verse. The lines added by the poet were superior, and the man who wrote the first two lines was said to have thrown a tile and drawn a piece of jade.

11. In a well-known Zen story, an old man told the Zen master Hyakujō that he had been a teacher in the past, but when a student asked if someone who is highly cultivated in meditation falls into the province of cause and effect, he denied it and became a "wild fox." Then the old man posed the same question to Hyakujō, who answered that someone who is highly cultivated "isn't blind to cause and effect."

Flowers in the Sky
(Kuge)

This essay is strongly colored with the Kegon doctrine of the inter-penetration of reality and illusion. Reality, in Kegon terms, means the interdependence of all things, which also means the "emptiness" of things in themselves. Particular emphasis is placed in this essay on counteracting nihilistic tendencies in the interpretation of emptiness and illusoriness: this may be noted time and again as one of Dōgen's persistent themes.

This point of emphasis is summed up in Dōgen's reversal of the focus of a traditional expression, "flowers in the sky." This term refers to that which is illusory or unreal; but where it conventionally had a negative connotation, Dōgen uses it here in a positive way. That is, instead of treating illusion as something to be annihilated, Dōgen points out that all is illusion, and being empty in its very essence is in that sense identical to absolute reality.

This is like saying that all existence is relative and therefore empty of absolutes, so to realize emptiness it is not necessary to annihilate existence. In fact, the very idea of annihilating presumes existence as something in itself real, hence is illusion within illusion. Dōgen points out that not only mundane things are "flowers in the sky," but so are the Buddhist teachings themselves. This might be said to be a funda-mental point of departure of Mahayana Buddhism, as articulated by the great dialectician Nāgārjuna a millenium earlier.

The essay begins with a famous line attributed to Bodhidharma, the alleged founder of Zen in China: "One flower opens with five petals, forming a fruit of its own accord." The "five petals" are traditionally thought to refer to the five Chinese patriarchs of Zen, or to the five houses of Chinese Zen. Dōgen points out these are multifold aspects of one "flower," while the "one flower" is the unfolding of these vari-ous aspects. Elsewhere in *Shōbōgenzō,* Dōgen emphasizes that the five houses or schools of Zen are not to be thought of as representing divi-sions or fundamental differences, and that Buddhism should be viewed not in a fragmentary, sectarian way, but as a whole comprising many different facets. This notion of Buddhism as a whole which is unified though various, various though unified, is also characteristic of the idea of "one vehicle" in the Kegon and Hokke teachings. Also like the Kegon, Dōgen here in his introduction emphasizes practice, symbolized by the flower, naturally bearing the "fruit" of realization. The metaphor of the flower and petals also can be extended to refer to the unity and multiplicity of all phenomena.

Next Dōgen goes on to bring up the classic symbol of the udumbara flower. This is a flower that blooms but once in three thousand years, a standard symbol for Buddha. Dōgen quotes an ancient saying that the udumbara flower blooms in "fire," suggesting that buddhahood is realized in the world. This emphasis on nondualism, on the cultivation and realization of buddhahood as being nowhere but in this life, is also typical of Dōgen; he carries this logic through to illustrate the interdependence of awareness and existence, and the identity of Buddha and existence itself.

Subsequently the essay proceeds to its main theme, the unity of existence and emptiness. The word for "sky" in the expression "flowers in the sky" is the same in Sino-Japanese as the word for the Buddhist term "emptiness," so this expression could also be read from Chinese as "empty flowers" or "flowers of emptiness." Dōgen stresses that everything without exception is "flowers in the sky." The traditional saying that "flowers in the sky" are due to cataracts or obstructions in the eye is here presented positively, with "cataracts" being used to refer to compassion, or nonextinction, the acceptance and recognition of life as it is. This positive interpretation of "sickness" is also characteristic of the popular *Vimalakīrti* scripture, in which "sickness" represents the sage's compassion and adaptive being in the world. Like that scripture, this essay by Dōgen is aimed at cutting through the notion of nirvana as opposite to mundane life.

Flowers in the Sky

The founder of Zen said, "One flower opens, with five petals, forming a fruit which ripens of its own accord."

One should study the time of this flower's blooming, as well as its light and color. The multiplicity of one flower is five petals, the opening of five petals is one flower. Where the principle of one flower comes across is *I originally came to this land to communicate the Teaching and save deluded sentient beings*. Where the light and color are sought must be this meditative study. It is *the forming of the fruit is up to your forming of the fruit*—this is called *ripening of its own accord*. *Ripening of its own accord* means cultivating the cause and experiencing the result. There is cause in the realm of common experience, there is result in the realm of common experience. Cultivating this cause and effect in the realm of common experience, one experiences cause and effect in the realm of common experience. *Own* is the self, the self is definitely *you*—it means the four gross elements and five clusters.[1] Because of being able to employ the *true human with no position*,[2] it is not "I," it is not *who;* therefore being *not compulsory* is called *on its own. Accord* is permission. *Ripening of its own accord* is the time of the flower's opening and forming fruit, it is the time of *communicating the Teaching to save deluded sentient beings*.

For example, it is like the time and place of the udumbara flower's blooming being in fire, during fire. Drilling for fire and flaming fire are both the place and the time of blooming of the udumbara flower. If not for the time and place of the udumbara flower, not a single spark of fire comes into being, there is not a single spark of life. Know that in a single spark of fire are a hundred thousand udumbara flowers, blooming in the sky, blooming on the ground, blooming in the past, blooming in the present. To perceive the time and place of the fire's appearance is to perceive the udumbara flower. We should not miss perceiving the time and place of the udumbara flower.

An ancient said, *The udumbara flower blooms in fire*. So the udumbara flower always blooms in fire. If you want to know *fire*, it is where the udumbara flower blooms. You should not, by clinging to views of humanity or views of heaven, fail to learn about *in the fire*. If you would doubt it, you should also doubt that lotus flowers grow in water; you should also doubt that there are flowers on branches. Also, if you must doubt, you should doubt the structure of the material world. Even so, you don't doubt.

If one is not a Buddha or Zen adept, one does not know *when a flower blooms the world comes into being*. *A flower blooms* is *in front, three by three, in back, three by three*.[3] In order to fulfill this number of members, all things are assembled and made grandiose. Invoking this principle, one can know the measure of spring and autumn.

But it's not that there are flowers and fruits in spring and autumn; *being time* always has flowers and fruit. Flowers and fruit together preserve time and season, time and season together preserve flowers and fruit. For this reason *the hundred plants*[4] all have flowers and fruits, all trees have flowers and fruits. Gold, silver, copper, iron, coral, and jewel trees all have flowers and fruits; earth, water, fire, air, and space trees all have flowers and fruits. Human trees have flowers, human flowers have flowers, *withered trees*[5] have flowers.

Among such as these existing, there are the *flowers in the sky* spoken of by the Buddha. However, those of little learning and little insight do not know what the colors, luster, leaves and blossoms of the *flowers in the sky* are like—they only hear of them as nonexistent flowers. Know that in the Buddha Way there is talk of *flowers in the sky*—outsiders don't know the talk about *flowers in the sky*, much less consciously understand it. Only Buddhas and Zen adepts alone know the blooming and falling of sky flowers and earth flowers, know the blooming and falling of world flowers, and so on, and know the sky flowers, earth flowers, world flowers, and so on are scriptures. This is the guideline for Buddhist study. Because that which Buddhas and Zen adepts ride on is *flowers in the sky*, the worlds of Buddhas as well as the teachings of the Buddhas are in fact *flowers in the sky*.

However, what ordinary ignoramuses think when they hear that the Buddha said what eyes with cataracts see are *flowers in the sky,* is that *eyes with cataracts* refers to the distorted eyes of sentient beings; they reason that since diseased eyes are distorted, they perceive nonexistent flowers in the clear sky. By clinging to this reasoning, they think it means falsely seeing as existent the nonexistent three worlds, six paths,[6] existent Buddhas, nonexistent Buddhas. They make a living on the idea that this says that if the deluding cataracts in the eyes were gone, these flowers in the sky would not be seen, and so there are originally no flowers in the sky. It is a pity that people like this don't know the time and season and process of the *flowers in the sky* spoken of by Buddha. The principle of the *cataracts in the eye, flowers in the sky* spoken of by Buddhas is not yet apparent to ordinary people and outsiders. The Buddhas, enlightened ones, cultivating these *flowers in the sky,* thereby *acquire the robe, seat, and room,*[7] attain enlightenment and realize its fruition. *Holding up a flower and winking*[8] is a public case where *cataracts in the eye, flowers in the sky* manifest. The *treasury of the eye of true teaching, the ineffable mind of nirvana,* correctly transmitted to the present without lapse, is called *cataracts in the eye, flowers in the sky.* Enlightenment, nirvana, the body of reality, inherent nature, and so on are a few petals of the *opening five petals* of *flowers in the sky.*

Shakyamuni Buddha said, "It is like someone with cataracts seeing flowers in the sky: when the affliction of cataracts is removed, the flowers perish in the sky."

There has not yet been a scholar who has understood this statement. Because they don't know *the sky,* they don't know the *flowers in the sky.* Because they don't know the *flowers in the sky,* they don't know *the person with cataracts;* they do not see *the person with cataracts,* do not meet *the person with cataracts,* are not *the person with cataracts.* One should meet *the person with cataracts,* know *the sky,* and see *the flowers in the sky* too. After seeing the *flowers in the sky,* one should also see *the flowers perish in the sky.* To think that once the *flowers in the sky* cease they should not exist anymore is the view of a small vehicle.[9] If the *flowers in the sky* were not seen, what would they be? (Those with the view of the small vehicle) only know *flowers in the sky* as something to be abandoned, and do not know the *great matter* after the *flowers in the sky*—they do not know the planting, ripening, and shedding of the *flowers in the sky.*

Ordinary scholars today think that where the sun energy abides is *the sky,* that where the sun, moon, planets, and stars hang is *the sky,* and due to that they think that saying *flowers in the sky* means the appearance of forms like floating clouds in this clear air, flying flowers blown hither and thither in the wind rising and falling. They are far from knowing that the creating and created four gross elements, all the phenomena of the material world, as well as fundamental enlightenment, fundamental nature, and so on, are called *flowers in the sky.* Also they do not know that the creative four elements and so on exist due to phenomena; they do not know that the material world remains in its normal state due to phenomena. They only see phenomena as existing due to the material world. They only realize that there are *flowers in the sky* due to *cataracted eyes;* they do not realize the principle that *cataract eyes* are caused to exist by *flowers in the sky.* Know that the *person with cataracts* spoken of by the Buddha is the originally enlightened person, the ineffably enlightened person, the person of the Buddhas, the person of the three worlds, the person beyond Buddha. Do not ignorantly consider *cataracts* to be delusive factors and thus study as if there were something else which is real—that would be a small view. If cataract flowers are delusions, the agent and action wrongly clinging to them as delusions would have to be delusions. If they are all delusions, there can be no logical reasoning. If there is no reason established, the fact that cataract flowers are delusions cannot be so.

In so far as enlightenment is a *cataract,* the myriad elements of enlightenment are all elements of a magnificent array of *cataracts,* the myriad elements of delusion are all elements of a grandiose array of *cataracts.* For now we should say that since *cataracted eyes* are equal, *flowers in the sky* are equal; since *cataracted eyes* are birthless,[10] *flowers in the sky* are birthless. Since all things are characteristics of reality, cataract flowers are characteristics of reality. It's not a question of past, present, and future, not a matter of beginning, middle, and end—because they are not blocked by origination and destruction, they are able to cause origination and destruction to be originated and destroyed. They originate in the sky and perish in the sky, originate in cataracts and perish in the cataracts, originate in flowers and perish in the flowers. All other times and places are also like this.

Study of *flowers in the sky* certainly has many grades. There is that which is seen by eyes with cataracts, there is that which is seen by clear eyes, there is that which is seen by the eyes of Buddhas, there is that which is seen by the eyes of Zen adepts, there is that which is seen by the eye of the Way, there is that which is seen by blind eyes. There is that which is seen for three thousand years, there is that which is seen for eight hundred years.[11] There is that which is seen for a hundred eons, there is that which is seen for measureless eons. Though these are all seeing *flowers in the sky,* since *sky* is of various kinds, *flowers* too are multifold.

You should know that *the sky* is *one plant*. This *sky* inevitably flowers, just as all plants flower. As an expression of this principle, the Buddha said there are originally no flowers in the sky. Although *there are originally no flowers,* where the fact that there are now flowers is concerned, the peaches and plums are thus, and the apricots and willows are also thus—it's like saying the *apricot trees yesterday had no flowers—the apricot trees in spring have flowers.* When the season arrives, flowers bloom—it must be the time of the flowers, it must be the arrival of the flowers. The precise moment of this arrival of the flowers has never been arbitrary. Apricot and willow flowers always bloom on apricots and willows—when you see the flowers you know they are apricots or willows; seeing apricots and willows, you can tell the flowers. Peach and plum flowers have never bloomed on apricots or willows—apricot and willow flowers blossom on apricot and willow trees, peach and plum flowers blossom on peach and plum trees.

The blooming of *flowers in the sky* is also like this—they don't bloom on any other plants or trees. Seeing the colors of the *flowers in the sky,* one assesses the inexhaustibility of the fruits in the sky. Seeing the blooming and falling of *flowers in the sky,* one should study the spring and autumn of the *flowers in the sky*. The spring of *flowers in the sky* and the spring of other flowers must be equal. Just as flowers in the sky are various, the time of spring must also be such. For this reason there exists spring and autumn of all time. To learn that *flowers in the sky* are not real but other flowers are real is ignorance of the Buddha's teaching. Hearing it said that there are originally no flowers in the sky, if one takes it to mean that *flowers in the sky* which were originally nonexistent now exist, it would be shallow thinking and small insight—one should go on to think in a more far-reaching way. A Zen adept said, "The flowers have never been born." The manifestation of this message is, for example, the principle of *the flowers have never been born, and never perish; the flowers have never been flowers, the sky has never been the sky.* There should be no inanity about existence or nonexistence confusing the context of the time of the flowers. It is like flowers always being imbued with colors: the colors are not necessarily limited to flowers, and the times also have colors such as green, yellow, red, and white. Spring brings on flowers, flowers bring on spring.

A certain scholar was a lay disciple of the Zen master Sekisō. He composed a verse on awakening to the Way which said:

Light shines silently throughout infinity

This light has newly manifested the monks' hall, the buddha shrine, the pantry, and the monastery gate. *Throughout infinity* is the manifestation of the light, it is the light of manifestation.

All conscious beings, ordinary and wise, are my family

It is not that there are not ordinary folk and sages—but don't slander ordinary people and sages because of this.

A single thought unborn, the totality of being manifests

Each thought is individual; this is certainly unborn.[12] This is the totality of being, totally manifest. Therefore he expressed this as *a single thought unborn.*

As soon as the six sense faculties stir they are blocked by clouds

Though the six sense faculties are eye, ear, nose, tongue, body, and mind, they are not necessarily two times three—they must be *three by three, before and behind.* *Stirring* is like the polar mountain, it is like the earth, it is like the six senses, it is like *as soon as they stir.* Since *stirring* is like the polar mountain, not stirring is also like the polar mountain. For example, it is making clouds and rain.

Removing afflictions doubly increases illness

It is not that there has been no illness hitherto; there is the illness of Buddha, the illness of Zen adepts. This knowledge and removal is doubling illness, increasing illness. At the very moment of removing, certainly that is affliction; they are simultaneous, they are not simultaneous. The fact is that afflictions always include the way to remove them.

Aiming for thusness is also wrong

Turning away from thusness is wrong, aiming for thusness is also wrong. *Thusness* is aiming for and turning away; in the individuality of each, aiming for and turning away, this is *thusness.*[13] Who would have known this *wrong* is also thusness!

Going along with the conditions of the world, without hindrance

Conditions of the world going along with conditions of the world, going along is a condition of the world when going along—this is called *without hindrance.* As for hindrance and nonhindrance, one must learn while hindered by the eye.[14]

Nirvana and life-death are flowers in the sky

Nirvana is unexcelled complete perfect enlightenment; the resting place of the Buddhas and Zen adepts as well as the disciples of Buddhas and Zen adepts is this. *Life and death* is the *real human body.* Though nirvana and life and death are these things, they are *flowers in the sky.* The roots and stems, branches and leaves, blossoms and fruits, luster and color of the *flowers in the sky* are all the blooming of the *flowers in the sky.* Sky flowers also produce sky fruits and give out sky seeds. Because the triple world we now perceive is the *five petals opening* of the *flowers in the sky,* it is *not as good as the triple world seeing the triple world.* It is this *true characteristic of all things.* It is this *flower characteristic of all things. All things, ultimately unfathomable,* are flowers and fruits in the sky. You should study them as equal to the apricots, willows, peaches, and plums.

Zen Master Reikun, when he first called on Zen Master Kisō, asked, "What is Buddha?" Kisō said, "If I tell you, will you believe?" Reikun said, "How dare I not believe the true words of the teacher?" Kisō said, "You are it." Reikun said, "How can I preserve it?" Kisō said, "When there is a single cataract in the eye, flowers in the sky shower every which way."

This saying of Kisō, *when there is a single cataract in the eye, flowers in the sky shower every which way,* is an expression of preserving Buddha. Therefore, know that the *showering every which way of cataract flowers* is the manifestation of Buddha. The flowers and fruits in the eye-sky are the preservation of the Buddhas. By means of *cataracts* the eye is caused to manifest; manifesting sky flowers in the eye, it manifests the eye in the sky flowers. It follows that *when there are sky flowers in the eye, one cataract showers every which way,* and *when one eye is in the sky, myriad cataracts shower every which way.* Because of this, *cataracts too are the manifestation of the whole works, the eye too is the manifestation of the whole works, the sky too is the manifestation of the whole works, the flowers too are the manifestation of the whole works. Showering every which way* is *a thousand eyes;* it is *eyes throughout the body.*[15] In whatever time and place there is an eye, there are inevitably *flowers in the sky,* there are *flowers in the eye.* Flowers in the eye are called flowers in the sky—the expression of flowers in the eye must be open and clear.

Great Master Kōshō said, "What a marvel! The Buddhas of the ten directions are basically flowers in the eye. If you want to know the flowers in the eye, they are basically the Buddhas of the ten directions. If you want to know the Buddhas of the ten directions, they are not the flowers in the eye; if you want to know the flowers in the eye, they are not the Buddhas of the ten directions. If you understand this, the fault is in the Buddhas of the ten directions. If you don't understand, a disciple does a dance, a self-awakened one puts on makeup."

You should know that it is not that the Buddhas of the ten directions are not real—they are basically *flowers in the eye.* The place where the Buddhas of the ten directions are in their position is *in the eye.* If it is not *in the eye* it is not the abode of the Buddhas. *Flowers in the eye* are not nonexistent, not existent, not void, not substantial—they are of themselves *the Buddhas of the ten directions.*

Now if you just want to know *the Buddhas of the ten directions,* it is not the *flowers in the eye,* and if you just want to know the *flowers in the eye,* it is not the *Buddhas of the ten directions*—this is how it is. Because it is this way, understanding and not understanding are both *flowers in the eye,* are *the Buddhas of the ten directions. Want to know* and *are not* are the marvel of manifestation, are a great marvel. The doctrine of sky flowers and earth flowers spoken by all Buddhas and Zen adepts is such a *flashing of style.* Though even teachers of the scriptures and treatises have heard of the name of *flowers in the sky,* when it comes to the life pulse of earth flowers there are no conditions for any but Buddhas and Zen adepts to see or hear of them. Knowledge of the life pulse of the earth flowers is captured in the sayings of the Buddhas and Zen adepts.

Zen Master Etetsu of Mt. Sekimon in China was an adept in the line of Ryōzan. A monk asked him, "What is the jewel in the mountain?" The point of this question is the same as asking, for example, what Buddha is; it is like asking what the Path is. The master said, "Sky flowers emerge from the earth; the whole country has no way to buy." This statement should not be considered on a par with others at all. Usually when Zen teachers talk about flowers in the sky, they only say they originate *in the sky* and then perish *in the sky.* None have yet known *from the sky,* much less *from the earth*—only Sekimon alone knew. "From the earth" is *beginning, middle, and end* ultimately *from the earth. Emerge* means *bloom.* At this precise time, they *emerge from the whole earth,* they *bloom from the whole earth. The whole country has no way to buy* doesn't mean that the whole country doesn't buy, it means that there is no way to buy. There are sky flowers that emerge from the earth, there is the whole earth that blooms from the flowers. Therefore know that *flowers in the sky* have the meaning of causing both earth and sky to bloom.

1243

Notes

1. "Four gross elements and five clusters" means the mental and physical elements of being.

2. "True human with no position" is a famous Zen expression referring to the ego-free human. See *Being Time,* note 8.

3. "In front, three by three, in back, three by three"—see *Blue Cliff Record,* case 35. Zen Master Hakuin says, "If you want to know how many this is,

you must know the number of last night's stars, the number of the drops of this morning's rain." It may be taken as referring to the totality of experience, differentiated in terms of appearances, characteristics, while equal in terms of essence.

4. "A hundred plants" means all things.

5. "Withered tree" refers to dispassion, disillusion. Dōgen's spiritual ancestor Tōzan spoke of Zen as "flowers blooming on a withered tree," or being in the world but not of the world.

6. The three worlds, or triple world, are the realms of desire, form, and formlessness. The six paths are the conditions of "animals" (delusion), "ghosts" (greed), "titans" (anger), "hell" (delusion, greed, and anger), "humans" (social virtue), and "celestials" (abstract meditation). These terms are a way of summing the sphere of mundane, conditioned existence.

7. "Robe, seat, and room" is an expression from the *Hokke* scripture: the "robe" of Buddhas is conciliation and tolerance; the "seat" of Buddhas is the emptiness of all things; the "room" of Buddhas is compassion for all beings.

8. The Zen legend of the beginning of the Zen transmission is that once before an assembly Shakyamuni Buddha said nothing but held up a flower and winked—no one understood but the chief disciple Mahā-Kāśyapa, who smiled. Buddha said, "I have the treasury of the eye of true teaching, the ineffable mind of nirvana, the true form, which is formless—this I hand on to Mahā-Kāśyapa."

9. The "small vehicle" of Buddhism emphasizes individual liberation, and its realization is sometimes referred to as "extinguishing cognition and reducing the body to ashes." It is contrasted to the so-called great vehicle, which emphasizes universal liberation, in that it is aimed at annihilating illusion whereas the great vehicle holds that illusion and enlightenment are not separate, and tries to attain liberation through comprehending illusion in both form and essence.

10. "Birthless" is used to mean "empty" in the sense of having no independent existence; accordingly, it also refers to the notion of the beginningless, endless, inextricable interrelation of all phenomena.

11. "Eight hundred" and "three thousand" are a pair of numbers commonly used in Zen talk to refer to indefinite multiplicity.

12. The sense of "unborn" here means every moment is unique; from the point of view of the moment, considering the moment in itself, there is no before or after in the present moment itself.

13. Var. lect. "In each of the aiming for and turning away that have aiming for and turning away from thusness, this is thusness." Thusness is all-inclusive. Those who try to aim for it, or who turn away from it, miss it in terms of conscious realization, but nevertheless are still part of thusness, and so are their efforts.

14. "Hindered" here means existence; being "hindered" by the eye means experiencing through the eye.

15. See *The Ocean Seal Concentration,* note 9.

The Ocean Seal Concentration
(Kai-in zammai)

The "ocean seal concentration," or, as it is sometimes rendered, the "oceanic reflection concentration," is said to be the concentration from which the Kegon scripture emerged, abruptly revealing the vast panorama of the Buddha's enlightenment. The treatise *Return to the Source Contemplation,* a Kegon work popular in Chinese Zen schools, says, "The 'ocean seal' is the fundamental awareness of true thusness. When delusion ends, the mind is clear and myriad forms simultaneously appear. It is like the ocean: due to wind there arise waves; if the wind stops the ocean water is calm and clear, and all images can reflect in it." Thus, in terms of mind, the ocean seal concentration may be said to refer to holistic, impartial awareness.

The twenty-fifth book of the *Ratnakūṭa* scripture says, "Just as all streams enter the ocean, all phenomena enter the seal of phenomena, hence the name oceanic seal." The "seal of phenomena," or "seal of law," refers to the treble seal of Buddhism. The twenty-second book of the *Treatise on Great Transcendent Wisdom* says, "The seal of law of Buddhism is threefold: first, all compounded things are born and perish from moment to moment, all are impermanent; second, all things are selfless; third is silent, extinct nirvana." The twentieth book of the same treatise says, "If one thinks in a discriminatory way, this is the net of the devil; not being moved and not remaining based on this is the seal of the law."

In this essay Dōgen introduces the ocean seal concentration by a paraphrase based on a passage from the scripture spoken by Vimalakīrti and the recorded sayings of the great master Baso. Following Baso, Dōgen cites the scripture in this way: "Only by the compounding of many elements (or phenomena) is this body made. At the time of its arising, only elements arise; at the time of its vanishing, only elements vanish." The strategy of analysis into elements is a traditional Buddhist device to dissolve the notion of intrinsic identity of the body (and mind) as a self or person; it also counters the notion of inherent identity of any compounded form. At the same time, in its broad application, this passage refers to the "body" of the universe as being a single compound or nexus of elements, a typical Kegon view; as Dōgen makes clear later, this seeing of the whole nexus is the ocean seal concentration.

The scripture as quoted by Dōgen goes on to say that the elements do not announce their arising and vanishing. This is like saying that they have no intrinsic identity. The notion of phenomena arising and vanishing depends on discriminating thought. In the terms of the treatise *Awakening of Faith in the Mahayana,* popular in both Zen and Kegon schools, awareness has two aspects: awareness of thusness and awareness of birth and death. Delusion means being trapped in the latter, in discriminating thought, which singles out things as discrete entities and thus is a linear, sequential way of perceiving, marking beginnings and ends. This is called delusion when it is believed—implicitly or explicitly—to be all there is, to be the only way of seeing, to be the true description of reality. This kind of awareness is by nature restrictive and exclusive (and for that reason may be useful and practically necessary at times while being harmful and counterproductive at others); to put it in a wider perspective the awareness of *thusness* (being-as-is, without conceptual glosses) is cultivated in Buddhism. Ultimately, enlightenment includes both aspects, so that one is neither forced to feel that thought and discrimination reveal the whole of reality, nor rendered incapable of orderly perception and discursive reasoning.

The final portion of the scriptural passage hints at the method of arriving at this synthesis: "Prior moment, succeeding moment—each successive moment does not await the next: prior element, succeeding element—the elements do not await each other. This is called the ocean seal concentration." The word "moment" also can be rendered as "thought," and in Sanskrit texts the term "thought-moment" or "mental moment" is often found. The point, as it applies to Zen meditation, seems to be awareness of the flux of moments without clinging, without stopping to bind them mentally into fixed structures or images. Thus, without the attention being caught up or dwelling on anything conceptually specified, the holistic awareness remains free and unobscured while the flow of events is clearly and impartially reflected therein. In the latter part of the essay Dōgen goes on to bring up further quotations and allusions from scriptures and Zen lore to develop illustrations of awareness and ways of fostering meditation to arrive at consciousness of the immediate totality.

The Ocean Seal Concentration

In being Buddhas and Zen adepts, it is necessary to be the *ocean seal concentration*. In swimming in this concentration, there is a time of speaking, a time of experiencing, a time of acting. The virtue of traveling on the ocean involves travel on the very bottom; this is traveling on the ocean as being *travel on the bottom of the deepest ocean*. Hoping to return *flowing in the waves of birth and death* to the source is not *what mental action is this?*[1] Though the passing through barriers and breaking divisions hitherto is originally each of the Buddhas and Zen adepts, this is the oceanic reflection concentration returning to the source.

Buddha said that only by the compounding of many elements is this body made. At the time of its appearance, only elements arise; at the time of its disappearance, only elements vanish. At the time these elements arise, they do not say "I arise," and at the time these elements vanish, they do not say "I vanish." Prior moment, succeeding moment —each successive moment does not wait for the next: prior element, succeeding element—the elements do not await each other. This is called the ocean seal concentration.

One should examine and meditate on this statement of Buddha in detail. Attaining the Way and entering into realization doesn't necessarily depend on much learning or a lot of talk. Broad learning still attains the Way in four propositions,[2] while thorough study of innumerable doctrines after all enters realization in a single line or verse. How much the more so of this statement—it is not seeking fundamental enlightenment in the future, nor is it bringing up initial enlightenment within realization.[3] Though causing the likes of fundamental enlightenment to become manifest is the virtue of Buddhas and Zen adepts, that does not mean that the enlightenments such as fundamental enlightenment and initial enlightenment are considered the Buddhas and Zen adepts.

The time of the so-called ocean reflection concentration is precisely the time of *only by many elements*. It is the expression of *only by many elements*. This time is called *compounding to make this body*. The *single compounded form* which has compounded many elements is *this body*. This is not taking the body to be one compounded form— it is a *compound of many elements;* it is expressing *compounding to make this body* as *this body*.

When it arises, only elements arise—this *elements arise* never leaves behind arising: therefore arising is not cognitive awareness, not knowledge or perception—this is called *they don't say "I arise."*[4] In not saying "I arise," it isn't that others perceive or cognize, think or discern that these elements arise. When meeting transcendentally there is indeed loss of opportunity in meeting. Arising is necessarily the arrival of the time, because time is arising. What is arising? It must be "arisen." This is already arising which is time, causing *skin, flesh, bones and marrow* to all be *revealed alone*. Because arising is the arising of formation by compounding, it is *only by many elements* which is the *this body* of arising, which is the *"I arise"* of arising. It is not just seeing and hearing it as sound and form; it is the *many elements* of *"I arise,"* it is the unspoken "I arise." Not speaking is not not expressing, because expression is not verbalization. The time of arising is *these elements,* it is not the twenty-four hours. *These elements* are the time of arising, not the simultaneous arising of the three worlds.

In ancient times the Buddha said, "Suddenly fire arises." The independence of this arising is expressed as *fire arises*. An ancient illuminate said, "How is it when arising and vanishing don't stop?"[5] So this *arising and vanishing* is unceasing *as we arise, we vanish*. This statement of not stopping should be comprehended positively by leaving it to itself. It causes this *time when arising and vanishing don't stop* to cease and continue as the life pulse of the enlightened ones. *When arising and vanishing don't stop* is *whose arising and vanishing? Whose arising and vanishing is it* is *to those who may be liberated by this body* . . . , it is *then manifesting this body* . . . , it is . . . *and teaching them*,[6] it is *the past mind cannot be found*,[7] it is *you have attained my marrow*, it is *you have attained my bones*[8]—because it is *whose arising and vanishing*.

"When these elements vanish, they don't say 'I vanish' "—indeed, the time of *they don't say "I vanish"* is *when these elements vanish.* Vanishing is the vanishing of elements; though it is vanishing, it must be elements. Because they are elements, they are not adventitious defilements; because they are not adventitious defilements, they don't defile. Precisely this nondefilement is the Buddhas and Zen adepts. *You too are thus,* (a Zen patriarch) says—who might not be you? This is because the preceding moment and the succeeding moment are both *I.* In this vanishing are arrayed many *hands and eyes*[9]—referred to as "unexcelled great nirvana," "this is called death," "clinging to it as annihilation," "being the dwelling place." That is to say, many such *hands and eyes* are, as they are, qualities of *vanishing.*[10] Though *not saying* at the time of vanishing being *I* and *not saying* at the time of arising being *I* have the *same birth* of *not saying,* they cannot be *not saying* having the *same death.*[11] Already it is the vanishing of the preceding elements, it is the vanishing of the succeeding elements, it is the preceding moment of the elements, it is the succeeding moment of the elements. They are elements preceding and succeeding momentary elements, they are the preceding and succeeding moments of the elements. *Not awaiting each other* are momentary elements, not relating to each other are elements. That which causes them not to be mutually relative and not to await one another is the expression of eighty or ninety percent. There is *letting go* and there is *gathering in* which make the four gross elements and five clusters of extinction into *hands and eyes.* There is progression and there is meeting which make the four gross elements and five clusters into the itinerary. At this time, *throughout the body is hands and eyes,* but yet it is not enough;[12] *all over the body is hands and eyes,* but yet it is not enough.[12] In general, extinction is a quality of Buddhas and Zen adepts. As for the fact that now there is this statement of nonrelation and nonawaiting, know that *arising* is arising in the beginning, middle, and end; it is a case of *officially not even a needle is admitted; privately, even a horse and carriage can pass.*[13] It is not making extinction await or relate to *beginning, middle, and end.* Even though elements suddenly arise where there has been extinction, this is not the arising of the extinct, it is the arising of elements. Because it is the arising of elements, they do not await each other.[14] Also it is not relating extinction to extinction. Extinction is also extinction of beginning, middle, and end. It is a case of *not bringing it forth when meeting, raising the idea you know it exists.* Even though there is suddenly extinction where there has been arising, it is not the extinction of arising, it is the extinction of elements. Though it may be the *this is* of extinction, though it may be the *this is* of arising, it is *just the ocean seal concentration being called myriad elements.* The cultivation and realization of *this is* is not nonexistent, it is *just this nondefilement is called the ocean seal concentration.* Concentration is actualization, it is expression, it is the nighttime when one *reaches back for the pillow.* The reaching for the pillow wherein the nighttime is *reaching back for the pillow* is not merely for billions and billions of eons—it is a case of *in the ocean I only expound the scripture of the lotus of the wonderful teaching eternally.*

Because it is *not saying "I arise,"* it is *I, in the ocean.* The preceding face is *eternally expounding,* which is *as soon as one wave moves, myriad waves follow;* the succeeding face is the *scripture of the lotus of the wonderful teaching* of *as soon as myriad waves move, one wave follows.*[15] Even though causing a thousand or ten thousand foot string to be rolled up and rolled out, what is to be regretted is its hanging straight down. The "preceding and succeeding faces" are *I, on the face of the ocean*—it is like saying the preceding point and the succeeding point. "The preceding point and the succeeding point" is *putting a head on top of the head. In the ocean* is not that there are people; *I, in the ocean* is not the abode of people of the world, it is not what sages love. *I alone am in the ocean*—this is the *expounding* of *only, eternally.* This *in the ocean* is not the province of in between, inside, or outside: it is *eternally expounding the scripture of the lotus of the wonderful teaching.* Though it is *not dwelling* in the east, west, south, or north, it is *the full boat empty, carrying the moon back.* This true return is *directly returning*[16]—who would say this is action lingering in the water? It is just manifesting actualization within the bounds of the Buddha Way, that is all. This is considered the seal that stamps water. Further, we say it is the seal that stamps mud. The seal that stamps water is not necessarily the seal that stamps the ocean; it must be the seal that stamps the ocean transcendentally. This is called the ocean seal, the water seal, the mud seal, the mind seal. Purely conveying the mind seal, it stamps water, stamps mud, stamps space.[17]

> Master Sōzan was asked by a monk, "I understand that in the teachings it says the great ocean does not lodge a dead body—what is the ocean?" Sōzan said, "It contains all existents." The monk said, "Why doesn't it lodge a dead body?" Sōzan said, "One void of breath is not attached." The monk said, "Since it contains all existents, why isn't one void of breath attached?" Sōzan said, "It is not that myriad existents are void of breath in effect."[18]

This Sōzan was a spiritual brother of Ungo; here the essential message of Tōzan was truly accurate. This *I understand that in the teachings it says* refers to the true teachings of Buddhas and Zen adepts; it is not the teachings of ordinary or holy people, it is not the small teaching of transmitting Buddhist doctrines. *The great ocean does not retain a dead body*—this so-called *great ocean* is not an internal ocean or an external ocean, and cannot be like the eight oceans. These are not what the student is questioning. It is not only recognizing what is not an ocean as the ocean, it is recognizing what is an ocean as the ocean. Even though one insist they are oceans, they should not be called the *great ocean*. The *great ocean* is not necessarily a ninefold abyss with salt water or something. *Many elements* must *compound to form*. How could the *great ocean* necessarily be merely deep water? For this reason, to ask *what is the ocean* is speaking of the *great ocean* because the *great ocean* is as yet unknown to humans and celestials. As for *not retaining a dead body, not retaining* must be *when light comes, striking light; when darkness comes, striking darkness*.[19] The *dead body* is dead ashes; it is *how many times encountering the spring without change of mind*. The *dead body* is something nobody has ever yet seen —that is the reason for not knowing.

Sōzan's statement *it contains all existents* speaks of the ocean. This expression of the essential message doesn't say that the one thing which is *who* contains all existents; it is *containing all existents*. It is not saying that the *great ocean* contains all existents; to say *it contains all existents* is simply the *great ocean*. Even though not being known as something, for the time being it is *all existents*. When *containing, though it be a mountain, it is not merely standing atop the highest peak; though it be water, it is not merely walking on the bottom of the deepest ocean.* *Gathering in* must be like this, *letting go* must be like this. The *ocean of buddha-nature,* the *ocean of Vairocana's treasury,*[20] are only *all existents.* Though the surface of the ocean is unseen, there is no doubt in the act of swimming along. For example, in Tafuku's speaking of a grove of bamboo, even if it is *one stem straight, two stems curved, three stems, four stems slanted,*[21] even if it is action causing *all existents* to be missed, why didn't he say it is a thousand curved, ten thousand curved, why didn't he say it is a thousand groves, ten thousand groves? We should not forget the principle that a single grove of bamboo exists in this way. Sōzan's saying *it contains all existents* is still *all existents.*[22]

As for the monk's saying, *Why is one void of breath not attached?* —while it is the face of mistakenly doubting, it must be *what mental activity is this?* When *I had hitherto doubted this fellow,* this is only meeting with *I had hitherto doubted this fellow.* In *what location?* is *why is one void of breath not attached,* it is *why doesn't it retain a dead body.* Here it is precisely *since it contains all existents, why doesn't it retain a dead body?* We should know that containing is not attachment; containing is *not retaining.* Even though all existents be a dead body, it must be the *simply requiring myriad years* of *not retaining.* It must be *the single expression of this old monk* of nonattachment. What Sōzan was trying to say with *it is not that myriad existents are void of breath in effect* is that whether all existents be void of breath or not, one must be unattached. Even though a dead body is a dead body, as long as there is practice which similarly learns from myriad existents, it must contain, it must be containing. The preceding process and the succeeding process, which are all existents, have their effect—this is not being void of breath. It is what is called one of the blind leading a group of the blind. The principle of one of the blind leading a group of the blind is, further, one of the blind leading one of the blind, it is a group of the blind leading a group of the blind. When it is a group of the blind leading a group of the blind, it is *containing all existents* being contained by *containing all existents.* In the Great Path one continues to travel on, if it is not all existents, its practice is not actualized—this is the ocean seal concentration.

1242

Notes

1. "What mental action is this?" is a Zen phrase which is often used to question apparently or actually arbitrary thought or action; or it may be used to question an intention or expression of thought or action without any presupposition.

2. The "four propositions" are existence, nonexistence, both, neither. These are said to underlie all human conception and to have fallacies which make it impossible for any one of them to be unequivocally true. On the other hand, defining existence as relative existence or conditional existence and nonexistence as emptiness of absolute existence, Buddhist logic shows how all of them can be both true and untrue, summing up the foundations of philosophy therein.

3. "Fundamental enlightenment" refers to the inherent buddha-nature which is said to be in all conscious beings; "initial enlightenment" refers to the realization of this nature. Upon initial realization, the distinction between fundamental and initial enlightenment disappears.

4. "*Elements arise* never leave behind arising"—that is to say, each moment is new, becoming is continuous: "therefore arising is not cognitive awareness, not knowledge or perception"—the direct experience characterized by "not leaving behind arising," or continual renewal, cannot be said to be cognitive awareness, knowledge, or perception because these are after-the-fact organizations of data recollected from the preceding moment of the ongoing flux; also they are indicative of subject-object dichotomy, which does not pertain in direct experience. Thus the nonidentification of arising elements refers to the immediate experience without conceptualization or labeling.

5. A monk asked Razan, "How about when arising and vanishing don't cease?" Razan said, "Tch! Whose arising and vanishing is it?" (or, "Who is it arising and vanishing?") (*Book of Serenity,* case 43)

6. The *Hokke* scripture's book on the "All-Sided One" says the embodiment of universal compassion manifests such and such bodies to people who can be liberated by such and such bodies, in order to teach them; that is, the enlightening beings, the bodhisattvas, appear in different forms according to the mentalities and potentials of the people they teach. Also, in a general sense, "reality" appears differently depending on the perceiver. So Dōgen uses "whose arising and vanishing is it" in a sense as an allusion to the relativity of perceiver and perceived.

7. The *Kongō* scripture says, "The past mind cannot be found (or grasped); the present mind cannot be found; the future mind cannot be found." The question "who?" is commonly used in Zen meditation to focus the attention in such a way as to lead to the actual experience of "the mind cannot be found." The singling out of the "past mind" here seems to direct the attention to unidentified immediate awareness.

8. "You have attained my marrow, you have attained my bones": according to Zen legend, when the Zen founder Bodhidharma was about to depart from China he called his four enlightened disciples together and had them reveal their understanding one by one. In responding to them, Bodhidharma said to the first, "You have attained my skin," to the second, "You have attained my flesh," to the third, "You have attained my bones," and to the last, "You have attained my marrow." The term *skin-flesh-bones-marrow* is often used by Dōgen, with the sense of the total being, the total experience or realization. Dōgen does not treat these four as different levels of understanding.

9. The bodhisattva, or enlightening being, personifying universal compassion is sometimes represented as having a thousand hands and eyes, to see and save all beings. Case 89 of the *Blue Cliff Record,* to which Dōgen repeatedly alludes in this essay, also is supposed to deal with totality: Ungan asked Dōgo, "What does the bodhisattva of great compassion do with so many hands and eyes?" Dōgo said, "It's like someone reaching back for the pillow in the night." Ungan said, "I understand." Dōgo said, "How?" Ungan said, "All over the body is hands and eyes." Dōgo said, "You've said quite a bit, but you've said only eighty percent." Ungan said, "What do you say?" Dōgo said, "Throughout the body are hands and eyes."

10. "Vanishing" is a word used for "extinction" and "nirvana." In the subsequent text "extinction" is used instead of "vanishing" for convenience.

11. Emptiness ("not saying") is the relativity or conditionality of phenomena, which arise and pass away; hence the temporarily existent and and the no longer existent are the same in terms of emptiness *qua* relativity, but emptiness *qua* relativity is not the same as annihilation.

12. Instead of "not enough," there is a variant reading "not it." Emotional interpretations, or clinging to the side of existence, are not right. See the verse and commentary to case 89 of the *Blue Cliff Record.*

13. This means everything exists conditionally ("privately") while nothing exists absolutely ("officially"). It also means wisdom, seeing through everything, doesn't cling to anything, but compassion may use any appropriate means for enlightenment.

14. Var. lect. "They are not relative to the characteristic of awaiting." Non-relation and nonawaiting refer in a way to both conventional and absolute reality: provisionally, things seem to be discrete; absolutely, there is nothing in essence to relate to or await, because there is no intrinsic reality in elements.

15. This passage can be interpreted in terms of both the Kegon and Hokke teachings. According to Kegon philosophy, the interrelation and interdependence of all things means that the unit implies the manifold and the manifold

implies the unit—so "when one wave moves, myriad follow; when myriad waves move, one follows." Another interpretation would be to take "one" in a totalistic sense: the one whole contains many elements, many elements make one whole. On this pattern, the first part (myriad following one) represents the Kegon teaching while the second (one following myriad) represents the Hokke. That is, the Kegon, which is represented as the eternal teaching of all Buddhas as manifestations of the cosmic Buddha, emphasizes many teachings emerging from the holistic realization of Buddha; the Hokke teaching, which is called "the lotus of the wonderful teaching," emphasizes many teachings leading into the total enlightenment of Buddha.

16. *Annals of the Empty Hall,* a Zen classic of the Chinese parent of the Sōtō school, says in case 17: "Turning around the light of awareness to illumine within, you directly return: clearly arriving at the spiritual root, it is not grasping or rejection."

17. "Stamping mud, water, space": according to the Sōtō teacher Tenkei Denson, "Though we divide it into three seals according to the potential of people with greater, middling, and lesser faculties, really it is the Great Way which has one stamp—there is nothing else at all. If you stamp space, there is no clue or trace; if you stamp water, there seems to be some clue; if you stamp mud, the pattern appears evident." (Hekiganroku Kōgi)

18. This translation is based on a truncated quotation as it appears in some texts of *Shōbōgenzō.* Other versions have a fuller quote, but this truncated version seems to be the form in which Dōgen intended to use it, to convey the notion that nonattachment does not mean annihilation. Cutting a quote to produce something quite different from the original is something Dōgen does at times when it fits his purpose.

19. This passage refers to eliminating attachments to differentiation and nondifferentiation, to being and nonbeing.

20. Vairocana is the main Buddha of the Kegon scripture, representing cosmic buddhahood; the ocean of Vairocana stands for the cosmos, as described in the Kegon scripture.

21. A monk asked Tafuku, "What is Tafuku's one grove of bamboo?" Tafuku said, "One stem, two stems, slanted." The monk said, "I don't understand." Tafuku said, "Three stems, four stems, curved." (*Transmission of the Lamp,* vol. 11)

22. Var. lect. "is still the great ocean."

The Scripture of Mountains and Waters
(Sansuikyō)

This essay presents an intricate, highly symbolic study of the inter-penetration of phenomenal existence and emptiness. It is characteristic of Zen writing that something may be used both as a metaphor and at face value in the same text, even in the same passage or the same word. In this essay, a most interesting pattern is revealed by taking "mountains" as a symbol of phenomena or existence, and "waters" as a symbol of noumenon or emptiness. These symbolic values, which have precedent in Chinese Zen literature, bring out the coherence of the essay. Because of the interpenetration, or interidentification, of existence and emptiness, the "mountains" and "waters," while primarily representing existence and emptiness respectively, each individually present both existence and emptiness as well.

The essay begins by stating that "mountains and waters" are the way of enlightenment; in essence both are beyond conception. It goes on to emphasize that the way to transcendence or liberation is none other than the "mountains"—this world. To counter the naive notion of phenomena as fixed entities, Dōgen then points out by means of Zen anecdote that while phenomenal existence abides, it is always in flux.

Attacking the limitations of fixed views, Dōgen contrasts the infin-ity of reality with the restriction of discriminatory thought. Through-out this essay he demonstrates shifting of perspective, to focus on exis-tence, emptiness, emptiness in existence, existence in emptiness, and their fundamental unity. While this is often thoroughly implicit and embedded in symbolic language, Dōgen also approaches the inter-penetration of emptiness and existence more explicitly and analyti-cally through examination of relativity among objects and between subject and object. The former approach is characteristic of the Sanron school of Buddhism, the latter of the Yuishiki school, while both are included in the Tendai and Kegon schools. In this connection Dōgen also pauses to denounce the contention that emptiness has no logic or reason, a view characteristic of immature or degenerate Zen theory.

In view of the length and complexity of this essay, specific explanations of significant transformations which may be obscure are provided in the notes. In general terms, Dōgen is concerned with dismissing the notion that things are just as one views them, the notion of emptiness as nothingness, the notion of permanence as constancy, and the notion of impermanence as annihilation. Thus dealing with the fundamental metaphysical bases of Mahayana Buddhism, the essay is aptly called a "scripture" in this sense as well as in the Kegon sense of "all things teach."

The Scripture of Mountains and Waters

The mountains and waters of the immediate present are the manifestation of the path of the ancient Buddhas. Together abiding in their normative state, they have consummated the qualities of thorough exhaustiveness. Because they are events *prior to the empty eon*,[1] they are the livelihood of the immediate present. Because they are the self *before the emergence of signs*,[1] they are the penetrating liberation of immediate actuality. By the height and breadth of the qualities of the mountains, the virtue of *riding the clouds*[2] is always mastered from the mountains and the subtle work of *following the wind*[2] as a rule penetrates through to liberation from the mountains.

Master Dōkai said to the congregation, *The green mountains are forever walking; a stone woman bears a child by night.*[3] Mountains lack none of the qualities proper to them. For this reason they *forever remain settled* and they *forever walk*. That quality of *walking* should be investigated in detail. Because the *walking* of mountains must be like the walking of people, don't doubt the *walking* of mountains just because it doesn't look the same as the walking of human beings. Now the teaching of the Buddhas and Zen adepts has already pointed out *walking*—this is the attainment of the fundamental. You should thoroughly examine and be sure about this indication to the congregation of *forever walking*—because of *walking*, it is *forever*. Though the *walking* of the *green mountains* is *fast as wind* and even faster, *people in the mountains* are *unaware, uncognizant*. *In the mountains is blooming of flowers* that is *inside the world*—and *people outside the mountains* are *unaware, uncognizant*. People who do not have the eyes to see the mountains do not notice, do not know, they do not see, do not hear—it is this principle.

If one doubts the *walking* of the mountains, one doesn't even yet know one's own walking either. It's not that one's own walking doesn't exist—it is that one does not yet know or understand one's own walking. If one knew one's own walking, one would know the walking of the green mountains. The green mountains are not animate, not inanimate; the self is not animate; not inanimate. One should not doubt this *walking* of the green mountains.

Who knows by the measure of how many phenomenal realms the *green mountains* may be perceived. The *walking* of the *green mountains* as well as the walking of oneself should be clearly examined. There should be examination both in *stepping back* and *stepping forward.*[4] *At the precise time* of *before signs,* as well as from *the other side of the king of emptiness,* in *stepping forward* and *stepping back, walking* never stops for a moment—this fact you should examine. If *walking* ever stopped, *Buddhas and Zen adepts would not appear.* If walking had a final end, *Buddhism wouldn't have reached the present. Stepping forward* has never stopped, *stepping back* has never stopped. When *stepping forward,* that doesn't oppose *stepping back,* and when *stepping back,* that doesn't oppose *stepping forward.* This quality is called the *mountains flowing,* it is called the *flowing mountains.* Because the *green mountains* too learn *walking,* and the *eastern mountains* learn *traveling on the water,* this *learning* is the *learning* of the mountains. This doesn't change the body and mind of the *mountains*—keeping the face of the *mountains,* they have *learned on a winding road.*

Don't repudiate this by saying that the green mountains cannot walk, that the eastern mountains cannot travel on the waters. It is because of the meanness of a low point of view that one doubts the saying *the green mountains are walking;* it is because of the incompetence of little learning that one is startled by the saying *flowing mountains.* While you don't even understand fully the words *flowing water* now, you are only sunk and drowning in small views and small learning.

So it is that the total bringing forth of amassed qualities is made into form and name, into the lifeline. There is *walking,* there is *flowing.* There is a time when mountains give birth to mountain children. Because of the principle of mountains becoming Buddhas and Zen adepts, Buddhas and Zen adepts emerge and appear in this way. Even when we may have eyes for the manifestation of *plants and trees, earth and stones, walls and fences,* we are not in doubt, not disturbed—this is not *total manifestation of being.* Even though a time may manifest when it is seen as *arrays of treasures,* this is not the true ultimate. Even if there is *manifestation of being* seen as the realm of the Buddhas' practice of the Way, it is not necessarily something to love. Even if we attain the summit of *seeing manifestation of being* as the inconceivable qualities of the Buddhas, reality as it is is not only like this. Individual views of being are individual objects and subjects. This is not to say that they are to be considered the *work on the Way* of Buddhas and Zen adepts—they are limited views of one corner. *Transforming the environment, transforming the mind* is something scorned by great sages; *speaking of mind, speaking of nature* is something not approved by Buddhas and Zen adepts; *seeing the mind, seeing nature* is the livelihood of heretics; *sticking to words and phrases* is not the expression of liberation. There is that which has passed through and shed such realms—that is *the green mountains are forever walking,* it is *the eastern mountains travel on the waters.* You should examine this thoroughly.

As for *a stone woman bearing a child by night,* the time when a stone woman bears a child is called *night.* Generally speaking, there are male stones and female stones, and there are stones neither male nor female;[5] they patch the sky and patch the earth. These are celestial stones and earth stones. Though this is a folk saying, it is rare for anyone to know it. You should know the principle of *bearing a child.* When *bearing a child,* do *parent and child emanate together?* Would you only approach the study of this in terms of child becoming parent being the actualization of bearing a child? You should study and penetrate how the time when parent becomes child is the *practice and realization* of *bearing a child.*[6]

Great Master Ummon said, *The eastern mountains travel on the waters.* As for the essential meaning of this expression of being, all mountains are *the eastern mountains;* all *the eastern mountains* are *traveling on the waters.* For this reason the manifestation, the experience of the nine mountains, Mt. Sumeru,[7] and so on is called *the east-*

ern mountains. But how could Ummon pass freely through the *skin, flesh, bones, and marrow,* the *livelihood of cultivation and realization* of *the eastern mountains?*

Now in China there is a type of incompetent, the number of which has grown so large that it cannot be countered by the small number of the genuine. They say that such stories as the one about *the eastern mountains* and the story of Nansen's sickle[8] are *stories without rational understanding.* Their idea is that stories involved with thoughts are not the Zen stories of the enlightened ones, and that stories without rational understanding are the stories of the enlightened ones. Therefore Ōbaku's caning[9] as well as Rinzai's shouting,[10] being unreachable by rational understanding and having nothing to do with thoughts, they consider to be the great enlightenment which is *before the emergence of indications.* The techniques of the worthies of the past are said to often use phrases which cut off complications—this is nonrational understanding. Those who talk this way have never met a genuine teacher, do not have the eye of meditation study; they are little ignoramuses who are not worth talking about. For the last two or three hundred years in China, baldheaded devil troops like this have been numerous. What a pity—the great Way of the Buddhas and Zen adepts is dying out. The interpretation of these people is not even equal to the listeners of the small vehicle; it is more stupid even than heretics. They are not lay people, not monks, not humans, not celestials. They are stupider even than animals studying the Buddha Way. The *stories without rational understanding* these baldies speak of have no rational understanding for them alone—it is not so of the Buddhas and Zen adepts. Just because they are not rationally understood by you, that doesn't mean you shouldn't study the road of rational understanding of the Buddhas and Zen adepts. Even if it should be *ultimately without rational understanding,* the rational understanding you are voicing now cannot reach it. People like this are numerous in the various Zen centers in China—I saw them with my own eyes. What a pity—they don't know that thoughts are verbal expressions, they don't know that verbal expressions transcend thoughts. When I laughed at them in China, they had nothing to say—they didn't say anything. Nothing but this false idea of no rational understanding. Who taught you this? Even if there is no teacher of natural reality, this is the heretical view of naturalism.

You should know that *the eastern mountains travel on the waters* is the *bones and marrow* of the Buddhas and Zen adepts. The *waters* have become manifest at the feet of *the eastern mountains;* for this reason the mountains climb to the clouds and walk in the heavens. The *top of the head* of *the waters* is *the mountains; walking,* both *heading upwards* and *right down,* is *on the waters.* The points of the feet of *the mountains* walk on *the waters,* cause *the waters* to spurt forth; so the *walking* is uninhibited, it is *not that there is no cultivation and realization.*

Water is not strong or weak, not wet or dry, not moving or still, not cool or warm, not existent or nonexistent, not delusion or enlightenment. When frozen, it is hard as diamond—who can break it? When melted, it is softer than whey—who can break it? Thus one cannot doubt the qualities it manifestly has.

For the time being you should study the time when you must look upon the waters of the ten directions in the ten directions. This is not the study of only when humans or celestials see water. There is the study of water seeing water. Because water *cultivates and realizes* water, there is the investigation of water expressing water. One should actualize the *way through* where self meets self. One should advance on the *living road* where other meets other, and should *leap out.*

Seeing mountains and waters has differences depending on the species. That is to say, there are those who see water as jewel necklaces; nevertheless, that is not seeing jewel necklaces as water. As what forms would we see that which they take to be water? Their jewel necklaces we see as water. There are those who see water as beautiful flowers; but they don't use flowers as water. Ghosts see water as raging fire, as pus and blood. Dragons and fish see palaces and pavilions. Some may see water as precious substances and jewels, or as forests and walls, or as the natural state of *pure liberation,* or as the *real human body,* or as the *characteristics of the body and nature of the mind.* People see it as water. It is an interdependency of killing and enlivening.[11]

It is established that what is seen differs according to the species. For the moment we should question this. Do you say that in viewing one object the views are varied? Do you say it is misapprehending multiple forms as one object? At the peak of effort one should exert further effort. Thus cultivation and experience, clarification of the Way, cannot be either one or dual; the ultimate sphere must be a thousandfold, ten thousandfold. In reflecting further on the basic meaning here, even though the types of water may be many, it is as if there were no basic water, as if there were no water of various kinds. However, the various waters according to the species (of perceiver) do not depend on mind, do not depend on body, are not born from actions, are not dependent on the eyes, do not depend on others—there is transcendence which *depends on water*.[12] Therefore *water* is not of the ranks of *earth-water-fire-air-space-consciousness*,[13] water is not blue, yellow, red, white, black, and so on, it is not form, sound, odor, flavor, feeling, phenomenon, and so on—yet nevertheless the water of *earth-water-fire-air-space-consciousness* is spontaneously manifested. Being so, one can hardly say for sure what the lands and dwellings of the present are producers or products of. To say they are resting in a sphere of space or an atmosphere is not the truth of self and not the truth of other—it is a proposal of the calculation of a small view. This statement comes from the idea that they cannot abide if they don't rest on anything.

Buddha said, *All things, ultimately liberated, have no abode.* You should know that although they are liberated and have no bondage, *all things dwell in their normative state.* This being so, when humans see water, there is a way of seeing it as flowing incessantly. That flowing has many kinds—this is one aspect of people's perception. It is said to flow through the earth, flow through the sky, flow upwards, flow downwards, flow through one bend, and flow in nine abyssal troughs. Rising, it becomes clouds; descending, it becomes pools.

In an old Confucian book it says, "The path of water is to become rain and dew when it goes up into the sky, to become rivers and streams when it descends to the earth." Even the saying of a worldly man was like this; for those who would claim to be descendants of the

Buddhas and Zen founders to be more ignorant than a worldling would be most shameful. What this says is that while the path of water is not yet consciously known by water, yet water does actualize it; while it is not that water is unaware, water does actualize its course. The book says *ascending to the sky, it becomes rain and dew*—you should know that water ascends to any number of skies and upper regions and makes rain and dew. *Rain and dew* are various according to the world. To say there is somewhere water doesn't reach is the teaching of the listeners of the small vehicle. Or it is the wrong teaching of heretics. *Water* reaches even into the flames of fire, it reaches even into thoughts, contemplations, and discriminations, and it reaches into awareness of the buddha-nature.

Descending to the earth, it becomes rivers and streams: you should know that when water descends to the earth it makes rivers and streams. The spirit of rivers and streams becomes wise people. Now what ordinary fools and common types think is that *water* must be in rivers, streams, oceans. That is not so. Rivers and oceans are made within *water,* therefore there is *water* even in places where there are no rivers or seas; when water descends to the earth it performs the function of rivers and seas, that's all. Also, you shouldn't get the idea that in places where water has formed rivers or seas there can't be worlds or buddha-lands there. Even in one drop infinite buddha-lands are manifest. So it is not that there is *water* in buddha-lands, and it is not that there are buddha-lands in *water.* Where *water* is has no relation to past, present, or future, no relation to the elemental cosmos. Yet even so, it is the *issue* of the *manifestation of water.* Wherever there are Buddhas and Zen adepts, there must be *water;* wherever there is *water,* Buddhas and Zen adepts must appear. Because of this, Buddhas and Zen adepts always bring up *water* as their body and mind, as their meditation. Therefore to say *water* doesn't rise on high is not in accord with either Buddhist or non-Buddhist classics. The *path of water* is to permeate *above and below, vertically and horizontally.*

However, in Buddhist scriptures, fire and air rise above, earth and water descend below. This *above and below* has a point to study. That is to study the *above and below* of the Buddha Way. That is to say, where earth and water go is considered *below*—it is not that *below* is taken to be the place where earth and water go. Where fire and air go is *above*—it is not that *above* is taken to be where fire and air go. Though the elemental cosmos doesn't necessarily have anything to do with measurements of direction, nevertheless, based on the action of the four, five, and six major elements, we temporarily set up an elemental cosmos of locations and directions. It is not that *thoughtless heaven* is above and *uninterrupted hell* is below—*uninterrupted hell* is the whole cosmos, *thoughtless heaven* is the whole cosmos too. Thus, when dragons and fish see water as palaces, it must be like people seeing palaces. They cannot cognize or see them as flowing anymore. If a bystander should tell them, "Your palaces are flowing water," the dragons and fish would be surprised and doubtful, just as we are when we now hear it said that the mountains are flowing. Yet they might maintain that there is such an explanation of the balustrades, stairs, and pillars of the palaces and pavilions. You should quietly ponder this treatment of the matter.

If you do not learn to penetrate freely beyond these bounds, you have not been liberated from the body and mind of ordinary people, you have not thoroughly investigated the lands of Buddhas and Zen adepts. Nor have you thoroughly investigated the lands of ordinary people, and they have not thoroughly investigated the palaces of ordinary people. Though now in the human world they have deeply ingrained cognition of what is in the oceans and rivers as water, they do not yet know what dragons, fish, and so on perceive and know and use as water. Do not ignorantly assume that what you perceive and know as water is used as water by all other species too. One should not linger only in the human realm—one should go on to study the *water* of the Buddha Way. As what do we see the *water* used by Buddhas and Zen adepts—one should study this. One should also study whether there is or there is not *water* in the house of the Buddhas and Zen adepts.

Mountains have been the dwelling place of great sages since beyond the past and beyond the present. Wise people and holy people both have made mountains their inner sanctum, have made mountains their body and mind; due to the wise and holy people, mountains have become manifest. Though it seems that so many great saints and great sages have gone into the mountains and gathered there, after having entered the mountains, there is not a single person who has met a single person—it is only a manifestation of the livelihood of the mountains. There are no further traces even of having entered.

In the time of gazing at the mountains while being in the world, the *crown and eyes* are far different from the time of meeting the mountains in the mountains. The idea of not flowing, and the cognition and view of not flowing as well, could not be equal to the cognition and views of dragons and fish. Humans and celestials find palaces in their own worlds; other species doubt this, or may not even get to the point of doubting. Thus you should learn about the saying *mountains flow* from Buddhas and Zen adepts—you should not give free reign to surprise and doubt. *Bringing up one,* it is *flowing; bringing up one,* it is *not flowing:* one time is *flowing;* one time is *not flowing.*[14] Without this exhaustive study, it is not *the Buddha's wheel of true teaching.* An ancient Buddha said, *If you want to be able not to elicit hellish karma, don't repudiate the Buddha's wheel of true teaching.* You should engrave this statement on your *skin, flesh, bones, and marrow.* You should engrave it on *body and mind, object and subject;* you should engrave it on *emptiness,* engrave it on *form.* It is engraved on *trees and stones,* on *fields and hamlets.*

Though mountains belong to the territory of the nation, they are entrusted to people who love the mountains. When mountains definitely love the "owners," saints, sages, and those of exalted virtue are in the mountains. When saints and sages live in the mountains, because the mountains belong to them, *the trees and rocks are abundant, the birds and beasts are holy.* This is because the saints and sages affect them with their virtue. You should know that the fact exists that mountains like sages and saints.

Many rulers have gone to the mountains to pay respects to sages and ask questions of great saints—this is an excellent example for past and present. When they do so, they pay respect to the saints as teachers, without following the ordinary laws of society. In the sphere of influence of wise rulers, there is no compulsion of mountain sages at all. It should be obvious that the mountains are apart from human society. In remote antiquity a chieftain went on his knees kowtowing to call on a sage in the mountains. Shakyamuni Buddha left the palace of his father the raja and went into the mountains, but his father didn't resent the mountains, nor did he suspect the people in the mountains who taught his son. Most of the Buddha's twelve years of training were in the mountains. The beginning of his teaching was also in the mountains. Truly even a supreme ruler doesn't coerce the mountains. Know that the *mountains* are not the realm of human society, not the realm of heavens. One cannot know or see the *mountains* by the measurements of human thought. If they did not take the flowing of the human world as the standard of comparison, who would doubt the *flowing of the mountains* or the *nonflowing of the mountains?*

Then again, since ancient times there have occasionally been sages and saints who live on the water. While living on the water, they have caught fish, they have caught people, they have caught the Way. All of these are ancient traditions of life on the waters. Advancing further, there should be catching oneself, there should be catching catching, there should be being caught by catching, there should be being caught by the Way.

In olden times monk Tokujō one day left Yakuzan to live on the river. Then he found the sage of Flower Inn River. Why not catch fish, catch people, catch water, catch oneself? Someone's getting to see *virtue and sincerity* is virtue and sincerity; *virtue and sincerity* making contact with someone is meeting someone.[15]

It is not just that there is water in the world; there are worlds in the realm of water. And this is so not only in water—there are also worlds of sentient beings in clouds, there are worlds of sentient beings in wind, there are worlds of sentient beings in fire, there are worlds of sentient beings in earth, there are worlds of sentient beings in phenomena, there are worlds of sentient beings in a single blade of grass, there are worlds of sentient beings in a single staff.[16] Where there are worlds of sentient beings, there must be the world of Buddhas and Zen adepts[17]—you should meditate on this principle very thoroughly.

So water is the palace of the true dragon.[18] It is not flowing. If you recognize it only as flowing, the word *flow* slanders water. That is because it is like insisting that it doesn't flow. *Water is just the true form of thusness* of water. The fact is that *water is the quality of water.* It is not *flowing.* In investigating the flow of one body of water and investigating *not flowing,* the *completed investigation* of myriad phenomena suddenly becomes apparent.

In the case of mountains too, there are mountains concealed in jewels, there are mountains concealed in marshes, there are mountains concealed in the sky, there are mountains concealed in mountains. There is study which *conceals mountains in concealment.*

An ancient Buddha said, *Mountains are mountains, waters are waters.* This saying does not say that "mountains" are mountains; it says mountains are mountains. Therefore you should investigate the mountains. If you investigate the mountains, that is meditation in the mountains. Such mountains and waters of themselves make sages and saints.

1240

Notes

1. These are standard Zen phrases meaning before or beyond conceptualization.

2. These are Taoistic expressions, here used to refer to freedom or transcendence.

3. "Stone woman" means a barren woman, but the term is rendered literally here for the sake of subsequent metaphor, since it does not alter the meaning. A stone/barren woman bearing a child refers to conditions without inherent nature producing interdependent origination. That is to say, phenomena, being conditional, have no absolute own-being, are not existent as independent entities. As "not existent," they are represented by the term "barren woman," which cannot produce. Yet in terms of conditional relations, things do exist—this is the "child." This is what is referred to by the Zen terms "really empty yet inconceivably existing." "Night" symbolizes emptiness, which is the identity of relative existence and absolute emptiness. The "mountains walking" alludes to the continual flux of the phenomenal, which temporally exists, but not as something static and fixed. This saying of Dōkai sums up the teaching of emptiness within existence and existence within emptiness.

4. "Stepping back" and "stepping forward" may be interpreted as contemplation of "existence is empty" and "emptiness is existence," respectively. The famed Sandōkai of Sekitō, a Chinese classic of Sōtō Zen, says, "Light and darkness are relative, like forward and backward steps." Experientially, stepping back and stepping forward can also be interpreted as, respectively, introspection and merging with the world.

5. Commentaries often refer to folk beliefs, but the point Dōgen seems to be driving at is that emptiness does not mean nondifferentiation in terms of characteristics; there is differentiation, but the differentiations are not absolutes. Hence "stone" may refer to emptiness in essence, "male and female" to characteristics of forms. Again this points to the nonduality of emptiness and form. Also, based on the ancient Zen terminology of "like a stone," used to describe the nonattached mind, this can refer to the ability to be unattached yet still active and versatile, able to appear and act in different ways without that action disturbing fundamental transcendence.

6. Child becoming parent and parent becoming child refer to the relativity of cause and effect—"cause" cannot be "cause" without "effect," by definition, so in a sense "effect" creates "cause." Generally, things are produced by conditions, but since the conditions must be interdependent, they cannot exist as conditions outside of their interrelation—so the "child," the interrelation, or product, is in that sense parent to the "parent" conditions. This type of reasoning was articulated by the Buddhist philosopher Nāgārjuna, to show the inconceivability of simultaneous interdependent origination in terms of linear logic. The specific manifestation of relativity which is illustrated by "child and parent" in the literal sense of the words is of course also possible here.

7. The nine mountains and Mt. Sumeru allude to an ancient Indian image of the world which was incorporated into Buddhist lore.

8. Nansen was working on the mountainside when a monk stopped and asked him, without realizing who he was, the way to Master Nansen's place. Nansen held up his sickle and said, "I bought this sickle for thirty coins." The monk said, "I didn't ask about the sickle—which way is it to Nansen?" Nansen said, "I use it real fast."

9. Thrice Rinzai asked Ōbaku the meaning of Buddhism, and Ōbaku hit him each time. Later someone told Rinzai that Ōbaku was just trying to relieve him of his distress (by halting his seeking mind), and upon hearing this Rinzai was enlightened.

10. Rinzai was famous for using shouts in his teaching activity. He said sometimes his shout was like a probe, sometimes like a cutting sword, sometimes like a crouching lion, and sometimes not used as "a shout."

11. What something "is" or "is not" (appears to be or does not appear to be) in the terms of the perceiver is a dependent matter. "Killing" means denial or nonbeing, "enlivening" means affirmation or being. The phenomenon of seeing things in different ways denies the absoluteness or ineluctability of any particular way of perceiving, yet affirms the possibility of all perceptions there may be.

12. This refers to the emptiness of own-being of water in noumenal terms, approached by repudiating the own-being of various waters in relations. In terms of the doctrine of emptiness—conditionality, emptiness is not itself something relative to existence, so there is no "basic water," taking "water" as a symbol for emptiness—"emptiness" is not itself something that exists. Furthermore, conditions do not have absolute existence, so there are no "various waters." The particular relative or conditional existents are usually said to depend on mind, or perception, and so on, but that refers to characteristics— here Dōgen is talking about essence, the very absence of own-being or inherent nature; this is the "transcendence which depends on water (emptiness)." In terms of Kegon philosophy, this is expressed by saying that form is empty (being relative), but the characteristics of form are not themselves the principle of emptiness.

13. These are the six major elements of the cosmos according to the description used in the Shingon school of Buddhism.

14. We may see the same actuality in terms of phenomenal characteristics (which flow) or noumenal emptiness (which does not flow).

15. I take this as a play on the name Tokujō, which literally means virtue and sincerity, saying that one can only see sincerity if one is sincere oneself, the contact with sincerity being what is called "meeting someone" in the Zen mind-to-mind sense of meeting. The fact that Dōgen uses the name Tokujō here instead of the nickname for this person—"The Boat Monk"—which is usually used, strengthens the case for taking it at its semantic value.

16. Each phenomenon is or contains various worlds according to the perception of various beings, the perception of each being in relation to the phenomenon being as it were a realm or a world.

17. According to the doctrine of Tendai Buddhism, the realm of buddhahood is latent in all realms of conscious beings.

18. "Dragons" are said to live in water, but here dragon is symbolic. The "dragon *samādhi*" represents being in the world and engaging in action without being fundamentally disturbed in mind; this can only be accomplished by realization of emptiness, because there is inevitably a limit to forced control.

Being Time
(Uji)

This essay has provoked the interest of most modern writers on Dōgen, presenting what seems to be his most original idea: the identity of being and time. This might be represented by the statement that time is a necessary factor of all manifestations of being. But Dōgen is less abstract. In effect, time here is seen as being concrete, being is seen as concrete, and the two are seen as inseparable in this concreteness.

Ordinary definitions of time, understood in terms of duration of objects or events, or as differentiations of velocity and distance, demand a concrete context, so the notion of the inseparability of being and time, arresting though it may be when expressed as *being-time,* is not especially difficult for the modern reader to acknowledge. What is more, Dōgen's idea of being time bears a degree of resemblance to the concept of space-time in the relativity theory of modern physics. In space-time, *time* is the fourth dimension, or fourth coordinate in terms of which, along with three spacelike coordinates, events are described.

One aspect of space-time is that the dimension of time is relative to the observer. In this essay Dōgen also shows how time may be seen in different ways—how, for example, "it passes from today to tomorrow, and passes from today to yesterday." That is, from the standpoint of looking forward and looking backward, time progresses from the present into the future, so that the passing present recedes into the past. This is the usual view of time. But then Dōgen goes on to say, "It passes from yesterday to today, it passes from today to today, it passes from tomorrow to tomorrow." The passage of time "from yesterday to today" is like its passage "from today to tomorrow" except that it refers to the future of the past instead of the future of the present. "From today to today" refers to the present of the present, each passing day being "today" from the vantage point of that day itself. "From tomorrow to tomorrow" refers to the future of the future, "tomorrow" as "the next day" never becoming today, but continuing to become "tomorrow."

This view of the relativity of time, one of the so-called ten mysteries of Kegon Buddhism, includes the notion of all things in all times always existing, in their respective times—that is, since their mutual relativity includes the relativity of their "time," they all exist at once without losing the order of their respective times. This view of the noninterference of linear time and "total" time is skillfully presented by Dōgen, and the essay demonstrates how particular manifestations of being are not only individual times but also part of the total fabric of the whole manifestation of being time. Thus all things and beings have their respective being times while simultaneously sharing in the being time of all existence.

While "being time" is one of the most, if not the most, striking and original presentations in Dōgen's thought, a survey of his entire work shows that he did not sloganize this expression or try to build a philosophy on this point per se. Rather, this essay on being time is another of Dōgen's versatile and lucid expressions of his more encompassing theme: the unity of being, and the misdirection of seeking or thinking of enlightenment outside the here and now.

Being Time

An ancient Buddha said, *At a time of being, standing on the summit of the highest peak; at a time of being, walking on the bottom of the deepest ocean; at a time of being, three-headed and eight-armed;*[1] *at a time of being, sixteen feet and eight feet;*[2] *at a time of being, staff and whisk; at a time of being, pillar and lamp;*[3] *at a time of being, the average man; at a time of being, earth and sky.*

So-called *time of being* means time is already being; all being is time. The *sixteen foot tall golden body* is time; because it is time, it has the adornments and radiance of time. You should study it in the twenty-four hours of the present. *Three-headed, eight-armed* is time; because it is time, it must be *one suchness* in the twenty-four hours of the present. The length and brevity of the twenty-four hours, though not as yet measured, is called twenty-four hours. Because the direction and course of their going and coming are obvious , people don't doubt them—yet though they don't doubt them, this is not to say that they know them. Because sentient beings' doubting of things which they don't know is not fixed, the future course of their doubting does not necessarily accord with their doubts of the present. It's just that doubting is for the moment *time*.

Self is arrayed as the whole world. You should perceive that each point, each thing of this *whole world* is an individual *time*. The mutual noninterference of things is like the mutual noninterference of *times*. For this reason there is *arousal of minds at the same time,* there is *arousal of times in the same mind.* Cultivating practice and achieving enlightenment are also like this. Arraying self, self sees this—such is the principle of *self* being *time*.

Because it is the principle of *being such,* there are *myriad forms, a hundred grasses*[4] on *the whole earth.* You should learn that each *single blade of grass,* each *single form,* is on *the whole earth.* Such *going and coming* is the starting point of cultivation of practice. When one reaches the state of *suchness*, it is *one blade of grass, one form*; it is *understanding forms, not understanding forms*, it is *understanding grasses, not understanding grasses.*[5] Because it is only *right at such a time*, therefore *being time* is all *the whole time. Being grass* and *being form* are both time. In the time of *time's time* there is *the whole of being, the whole world.* For a while try to visualize whether or not there is *the whole being, the whole world* apart from the present time.

In spite of this, when people are ordinary folk who have not studied the Buddha's teaching, the views they have are such that when they hear the expression *a time of being*, they think at some time one had become *three-headed and eight-armed*, at some time one had become *sixteen feet tall, eight feet seated*, like having crossed rivers and crossed mountains. They think, "Even though those mountains and rivers may exist still, I have passed them and am now in the vermillion tower of the jewel palace—the mountains and rivers and I are as far apart as sky and earth." However, the truth is not just this one line of reasoning alone. In the time one climbed the mountains and crossed the rivers, there was oneself. There must be *time* in oneself. Since oneself exists, *time* cannot leave. If time is not the appearances of going and coming, the time of climbing a mountain is the *immediate present* of *being time.* If time preserves the appearances of going and coming, there is in oneself the *immediate present* of *being time*—this is *being time.* Does not that *time* of *climbing mountains and crossing rivers* swallow up this *time* of the *vermillion tower of the jewel palace?* Does it not spew it forth?

Three-headed, eight-armed is yesterday's *time; sixteen feet, eight feet* is today's *time.* However, the principle of *yesterday and today* is just the time of directly entering the mountains and gazing out over the thousand peaks, the myriad peaks—it is not a matter of having passed. *Three-headed, eight-armed* too *transpires* as one's own *being time; sixteen feet, eight feet* too *transpires* as one's own *being time.* Though it seems to be elsewhere, it is *right now.* So pines are *time* too; bamboo is *time* too.

One should not understand time only as flying away; one should not only get the idea that flying away is the function of time. If time only were to fly, then there would be gaps. Not having heard of the path of *being time* is because of learning only that it has passed. To tell the gist of it, all existences in the whole world, while being lined up, are individual times. Because it is *being time,* it is *my being time.* In *being time* there is the quality of passage. That is, it passes from today to tomorrow, it passes from today to yesterday, it passes from yesterday to today, it passes from today to today, it passes from tomorrow to tomorrow.

Because passage is a quality of time, past and present time doesn't pile up, doesn't accumulate in a row—nevertheless Seigen is *time,* Ōbaku too is *time,* Baso and Sekitō also are *time.*[6] Since self and others are *time,* cultivation and realization are times. *Going into the mud, going into the water*[7] is similarly *time.*

Though the present views and the conditions of views of ordinary people are what ordinary people see, they are not the norm of ordinary people. It is merely that the norm temporarily conditions ordinary people. Because of learning that this *time,* this *being,* are not the norm, they take the *sixteen foot tall golden body* as not themselves. Trying to escape by claiming that oneself is not the *sixteen foot tall golden body* is also itself bits of *being time;* it is the *looking* of *those who have not yet verified it.*[8]

Even causing the horses and sheep now arrayed in the world to exist is the *rising and falling, ups and downs* which are the *suchness* of *remaining in the normal position.*[9] The *rat* is time, the *tiger* is time too.[10] Living beings are time. Buddhas are time too. This *time* witnesses the whole world with *three heads and eight arms,* it witnesses the whole world with *the sixteen foot tall golden body.*

Now exhausting the limits of the whole world by means of the whole world is called investigating exhaustively. To actualize being *the sixteen foot golden body* by means of *the sixteen foot golden body* as determination, cultivating practice, enlightenment, and nirvana, is *being,* is *time.* Just investigating exhaustively *all time* as *all being,* there is nothing left over. Because leftovers are leftovers, even the *being time* of half-exhaustive investigation is the exhaustive investigation of half *being time.*[11]

Even forms which seem to slip by are *being.* Furthermore, if you leave it at that, being the period of manifestation of *slipping by,* it is the *abiding in position* of *being time.* Don't stir it as nonexistence, don't insist on it as existence. Only conceiving of time as passing one way, one doesn't understand it as not yet having arrived. Though understanding is *time,* it has no relation drawn by another.[12] Only recognizing it as coming and going, no skin bag[13] has seen through it as *being time* of *abiding in position*—how much less could there be a time of *passing through the barrier?* Even recognizing *remaining in position,* who can express the preservation of *already being such?* Even if they have long expressed it as *such,* still everyone gropes for the appearance of its countenance. If we leave ordinary people's being *being time* at that, then even enlightenment and nirvana are only *being time* which is merely the appearances of going and coming.

In sum, it cannot be ensnared or arrested—it is the manifestation of *being time.* The celestial monarchs and celestial beings manifesting in the regions right and left are *being time* now exerting their whole strength. The other myriad *being times* of water and land are now manifesting exerting their whole strength. The various species and objects that are *being time* in darkness and light are all the manifestation of their whole strength, they are the passage of their total strength. If they were not the present *passage of whole strength,* not one single thing would become manifest, there would be no passage— you should study it this way. You should not have been learning about passage as like the wind and rain's going east and west. The *whole world* is not *inactive,* it is not *neither progressing nor regressing:* it is *passage.*

Passage is, for example, like spring: in spring there are numerous appearances—this is called *passage.* You should learn that it *passes through* without any external thing. For example, the *passage* of spring necessarily *passes through* spring. Though *passage* is not spring, because it is the *passage* of spring, *passage* has *accomplished the Way* in this *time* of spring. You should examine thoroughly in whatever you are doing. In speaking of *passage,* if you think that the objective realm is outside and the phenomenon which *passes through*

passes a million worlds to the east through a billion eons, in thinking thus you are not concentrating wholly on the study of the Buddha Way.

Yakuzan, at the direction of the Zen master Sekitō, went to call on
the Zen master Baso. He said, "As far as the Buddhist canon is concerned, I pretty much understand its message—what is the living
meaning of Zen?" When Yakuzan asked this, Baso said, "Sometimes I
have him raise the eyebrows and blink the eyes. Sometimes I don't
have him raise the eyebrows and blink the eyes. Sometimes having him
raise the eyebrows and blink the eyes is it, sometimes having him raise
the eyebrows and blink the eyes is not it." Hearing this, Yakuzan was
greatly enlightened. He said to Baso, "When I was with Sekitō, I was
like a mosquito climbing on an iron ox."

What Baso says is not the same as others. *Eyebrows and eyes* must
be *mountains and oceans,* because *mountains and oceans* are *eyebrows and eyes.* That *having him raise* must see the *mountains,* that
having him blink must have its source in the *ocean.* It is conditioned
by *him, he* is induced by causation.[14] *Not it* is not *not having him, not
having him* is not *not it.* These are all *being time.* The mountains are
time, the oceans are *time* too. If they were not *time,* the mountains
and oceans could not be. You should not think there is no *time* in the
immediate present of the mountains and oceans. If *time* disintegrates,
mountains and oceans too disintegrate; if *time* is indestructible, mountains and oceans too are indestructible. On this principle *the morning
star* appears, *the Buddha* appears, *the eye* appears, *the raising of the
flower* appears. This is *time.* If it were not *time,* it would not be thus.

Zen Master Kisei of Sekken was a religious descendant of Rinzai,
and was the heir of Shuzan. One time he said to the community,
"Sometimes the intent arrives but the expression doesn't arrive: sometimes the expression arrives but the intent doesn't arrive. Sometimes
intent and expression both arrive, sometimes neither intent nor
expression arrive." *Intent* and *expression* are both *being time; arriving*
and *not arriving* are both *being time.* Though *the time of arrival is
incomplete,* yet *the time of nonarrival has come. Intent* is a donkey,
expression is a horse; the horse is considered the expression, the don-

key is considered the intent. *Arriving* is not *coming; not arriving* is not *yet to come.* This is the way *being time* is. *Arriving* is blocked by *arriving,* not blocked by *not arriving. Not arriving* is blocked by *not arriving,* not blocked by *arriving. Intent* blocks *intent* and sees *intent; expression* blocks *expression* and sees *expression. Blocking* blocks *blocking* and sees *blocking. Blocking* blocks *blocking*—this is *time.*[15] Though *blocking* is used by *other things,* there is never any *blocking* which blocks *other things.*[16] It is *oneself meeting other people,* it is *other people meeting other people,* it is *oneself meeting oneself,* it is *going out* meeting *going out.* If these do not have *time,* they are not *so.*

Also, *intent* is the *time* of *the issue at hand; expression* is the *time* of *the key of transcendence. Arriving* is the *time* of *the whole body; not arriving* is the *time* of *one with this, detached from this.* In this way should you correctly understand and *be time.*

Though the aforementioned adepts have all spoken as mentioned, is there nothing further to say? We should say *intent and expression half arriving too is being time; intent and expression half not arriving too is being time.* There should be study like this. *Having him raise his eyebrows and blink his eyes is half being time; having him raise his eyebrows and blink his eyes is amiss being time. Not having him raise his eyebrows and blink his eyes is half being time; not having him raise his eyebrows and blink his eyes is amiss being time.*[17] To investigate thus, coming and going, investigating arriving and investigating not arriving, is the *time* of *being time.*

1240

Notes

1. "Three-headed and eight-armed" is the form of a titan, representing wrath.

2. The idealized or glorified body of Buddha, representing higher development of humanity, is referred to as being sixteen feet tall standing and eight feet high seated.

3. "Staff and whisk," "pillar and lamp," are often used in Zen lore to stand for objects or phenomena in general.

4. "Hundred grasses," or hundred plants, is a conventional term for all things or all forms.

5. "Understanding" and "not understanding" refer, respectively, to the realm of phenomena and appearances and the realm of noumenon or emptiness. Clarifying and sharpening relative understanding while at the same time being aware of the ultimate inconceivability of existence in itself is a Zen art.

6. Seigen, Ōbaku, Baso, and Sekitō were all famous Chinese Zen adepts of the eighth to ninth centuries.

7. "Going into mud and water" is a standard expression for entering the world, often used to refer to one who has transcended the world, then willingly acting in the world for an instructive purpose.

8. Rinzai said, "In this naked mass of flesh is a true human with no position or rank, always coming in and going out through the senses. Those who have not yet witnessed it, look!"

9. "Remaining in the normal position," or abiding in the normative state, is a phrase from the Hokke scripture often used by Dōgen. It means in effect that emptiness of absolute identity or unconditional existence does not negate relative identity or existence.

10. Rat and tiger are used to name particular times in the twelve-hour day of Sino-Japanese calendry, and as signs of the zodiac are also assigned to years in the twelve-year cycle.

11. "Leftovers being leftovers" seems to refer to noumenon and phenomena in terms of their separate identities as different aspects or facets of the totality of interdependent origination. Half-exhaustive investigation would be that of either noumenon (absolute emptiness) or phenomena (the realm of appearances and differentiation), the exhaustive investigation of either one being that of half being-time, as being-time is the totality of noumenon and phenomena.

12. Var. lect. "another time."

13. "Skin bag" means the mortal or physical being.

14. The living meaning of Zen ("it") as being time is conditioned, in its manifestation, by the person: the person is manifest according to causation (karma). This passage thus can be taken to mean that though the essence of Zen is in everyone, its expression, or realization, depends on personal cultivation.

15. Here "block" means being within a particular being-time; hence it says that states or things "block" themselves—this is in the sense of their being in, or being, their respective being-times.

16. The being in a particular being-time also defines ("is used by") other things by relativity: an individual being-time does not interfere with the being-time of anything else, however.

17. Again, emptiness and relative existence are each "one half"—if there is one-sided clinging to emptiness ("not raising the eyebrows") or existence ("raising the eyebrows"), this is "amiss."

The Eight Awarenesses of Great People
(Hachidaininkaku)

Ultimately, Buddhism is supposed to be practical, and its traditional reservation about philosophy is that in the excitement of intellectual exercise there is a tendency to forget that the teachings are meant to be applied. One of the great Buddhist teachers of China put it in these terms: first comes understanding, without which action is blind; then comes action, without which understanding is ineffective; finally understanding and action become one.

"Don't do any evil, do what is good, and purify the mind—this is the teaching of all Buddhas." This ancient formulation of Buddhism sums up the message of the final three chapters of *Shōbōgenzō* to be presented in this volume. Together they illustrate three fundamental phases or elements of Zen found throughout the whole of the Buddhist teachings: detachment, integration, and harmonization of detachment and integration.

The Eight Awarenesses of Great People, ostensibly written for mendicants but applying to lay people as well, may be considered a general outline of the main elements of Buddhist practice concerning detachment. The result, nirvana, is sometimes referred to as coolness, dispassion, noncontentiousness. The peace and mind and clarity thus realized are one facet of liberation.

The Eight Awarenesses of Great People

The Buddhas are great people. As these are what is realized by great people, they are called the awarenesses of great people. Realizing these principles is the basis of nirvana. This was the final teaching of our original teacher, Shakyamuni Buddha, on the night he passed away into final extinction.

1. Having few desires

Not extensively seeking objects of desire not yet attained is called having few desires.

Buddha said, "You monks should know that people with many desires seek to gain a lot, and therefore their afflictions are also many. Those with few desires have no seeking and no craving, so they don't have this problem. You should cultivate having few desires even for this reason alone, to say nothing of the fact that having few desires can produce virtues. People with few desires are free from flattery and deviousness whereby they might seek to curry people's favor, and they also are not under the compulsion of their senses. Those who act with few desires are calm, without worry or fear. Whatever the situation, there is more than enough—there is never insufficiency. Those who have few desires have nirvana."

2. Being content

To take what one has got within bounds is called being content.

Buddha said, "O monks, if you want to shed afflictions, you should observe contentment. The state of contentment is the abode of prosperity and happiness, peace and tranquility. Those who are content may sleep on the ground and still consider it comfortable; those who are not content would be dissatisfied even in heaven. Those who are not content are always caught up in sensual desires; they are pitied by those who are content."

3. Enjoying quietude

Leaving the clamor and staying alone in deserted places is called enjoying quietude.

Buddha said, "O monks, if you wish to seek the peace and happiness of quietude and nonstriving, you should leave the clamor and live without clutter in a solitary place. People in quiet places are honored by the gods. Therefore you should leave your own group as well as other groups, stay alone in a deserted place, and think about extirpating the root of suffering. Those who like crowds suffer the vexations of crowds, just as a big tree will suffer withering and breakage when flocks of birds gather on it. Worldly ties and clinging sink you into a multitude of pains, like an old elephant sunk in the mud, unable to get itself out."

4. Diligence

Diligently cultivating virtues without interruption is called diligence, pure and unalloyed, advancing without regression

Buddha said, "O monks, if you make diligent efforts, nothing is hard. Therefore you should be diligent. It is like even a small stream being able to pierce rock if it continually flows. If the practitioner's mind flags and gives up time and gain, that is like drilling for fire but stopping before heat is produced—though you want to get fire, fire can hardly be gotten this way."

5. Unfailing recollection

This is also called keeping right mindfulness; keeping the teachings without loss is called right mindfulness, and also called unfailing recollection.

Buddha said, "O monks, if you seek a good companion and seek a good protector and helper, nothing compares to unfailing recollection. Those who have unfailing recollection cannot be invaded by the thieving afflictions. Therefore you should concentrate your thoughts and keep mindful. One who loses mindfulness loses virtues. If one's power of mindfulness is strong, even if one enters among the thieving desires one will not be harmed by them. It is like going to the front lines wearing armor—then one has nothing to fear."

6. Cultivating meditation concentration

Dwelling on the teaching without distraction is called meditation concentration.

Buddha said, "O monks, if you concentrate the mind, it will be in a state of stability and you will be able to know the characteristics of the phenomena arising and perishing in the world. Therefore you should energetically cultivate and learn the concentrations. If you attain concentration, your mind will not be distracted. Just as a household careful of water builds a dam, so does the practitioner, for the sake of the water of knowledge and wisdom, cultivate meditation concentration well, to prevent them from leaking."

7. Cultivating wisdom

Developing learning, thinking, and application, the realization is wisdom.

Buddha said, "O monks, if you have wisdom, you will have no greedy attachment. Always examine yourselves and do not allow any heedlessness. Then you will be able to attain liberation from ego and things. Otherwise, you are neither people of the Way nor laypeople—there is no way to refer to you. True wisdom is a secure ship to cross the sea of aging, sickness, and death. It is also a bright lamp in the darkness of ignorance, good medicine for all the ailing, a sharp axe to fell the trees of afflictions. Therefore you should use the wisdom of learning, thinking, and application, and increase it yourself. if anyone has the illumination of wisdom, this is a person with clear eyes, even though it be the mortal eye."

8. Not engaging in vain talk

Realizing detachment from arbitrary discrimination is called not engaging in vain talk; when one has fully comprehended the character of reality, one will not engage in vain talk.

Buddha said, "O monks, if you indulge in various kinds of vain talk, your mind will be disturbed. Even if you leave society you will still not attain liberation. Therefore you should immediately give up vain talk which disturbs the mind. If you want to attain bliss of tranquility and dispassion, you should extinguish the affliction of vain talk."

These are the eight awarenesses of great people. Each one contains the eight, so there are sixty-four. If you expand them, they must be infinite; if you summarize them, there are sixty-four. After the final speech of the great teacher Shakyamuni, made for the instruction of the Great Vehicle, the ultimate discourse at midnight on the fifteenth day of the second month, he didn't preach anymore and finally became utterly extinct.

Buddha said, "You monks always should single-mindedly seek the path of emancipation. All things in the world, mobile and immobile, are unstable forms which disintegrate. Stop now and don't talk anymore. The time is about past, and I am going to cross over into extinction. This is my last instruction."

Therefore students of the Buddha definitely should learn these principles. Those who do not learn them, who do not know them, are not students of Buddha. These awarenesses are the Buddha's treasury of the eye of true teaching, the sublime heart of nirvana. The fact that many now nevertheless do not know them and few have read or heard of them is due to the interference of demons. Also, those who have cultivated little virtue in the past do not hear of or see them.

In the past, during the periods of the true teaching and the imitation teaching, all Buddhists knew them, and practiced and studied them. Now there are hardly one or two among a thousand monks who know the eight awarenesses of great people. What a pity—the decline in the degenerate age is beyond compare. While the true teaching of the Buddha is still current in the world and goodness has not yet perished, one should hasten to learn them. Don't be lazy. It is difficult to encounter the Buddha's teaching even in countless eons. It is also difficult to get a human body. And even if one gets a human body, it is preferable to live as a human where it is possible to see a Buddha, hear the teaching, leave the mundane, and attain enlightenment. Those who died before the Buddha's final extinction didn't hear of these eight awarenesses of great people, and didn't learn them. Now we have heard of them and learn them—this is the power of virtue cultivated in the past. Now, learning and practicing them, developing them life after life, we will surely reach unexcelled enlightenment. Explain them to people the same as Shakyamuni Buddha.

1253

The Four Integrative Methods of Bodhisattvas
(Bodaisatta shishōhō)

Bodhisattvas are people committed to the welfare, liberation, and enlightenment of all living beings; to dwell in detachment and cling to nirvana hampers this commitment, so they carry transcendence one step further. *The Four Integrative Methods of Bodhisattvas* restates a traditional Buddhist formulation representing nonselfish ways of being in the world. For bodhisattvas, absorption in the commitment of all bodhisattvas, becoming aware of the link of all beings and the eternal work of enlightening, is in itself a gateway of liberation from narrow selfish concerns.

The Four Integrative Methods
of Bodhisattvas

The four integrative methods of bodhisattvas are giving, kind speech, beneficial action, and cooperation.

This *giving* means not coveting; not coveting is not being greedy. In worldly terms it is said that not being greedy means not flattering. Even if one should rule four continents, to provide education and civilization in the correct way is just a matter of not being covetous. For example, it is like the treasures one relinquishes being given to strangers. To offer flowers from distant mountains to a Buddha, to give away treasures from one's past life to living beings—in terms of teaching as well as in terms of things, in each are inherent virtues involved in giving.

There is a principle that even if it is not one's own thing, that does not hinder giving. It doesn't matter how insignificant the thing is—the principle is that the effort must be genuine. When one leaves the Way to the Way, one attains the Way. When attaining the Way, the Way is necessarily being left to the Way. When goods are left to goods, the goods unfailingly become giving. Self gives to self, other gives to other. The causal power of this giving reaches afar, throughout the heavens and human world, and even reaches the realized sages and saints. The reason for saying this is that, having become the recipient of giving and having formed an affinity, the Buddha said on this account, "When a person who gives comes into a group, the people first look at that person. Know that heart implicitly comes across."

Therefore one should give even a single phrase or a single verse of the teaching. It becomes a good seed in this life and other lives. One should give even a single coin or a single blade of grass of resources—it causes roots of goodness in this age and other ages to sprout. Teaching too is treasure, material resources too are teaching. It must depend on the will and aspiration.

In fact, there are cases where one person effected the well-being of another by giving his whiskers, and someone gained kingship after having presented sand to a Buddha. They didn't crave the thanks of others, they just did what they could. Setting up a ferry or building a bridge is also transcendent generosity of giving. When one learns giving well, being born and dying are both giving. All productive labor is fundamentally giving. Entrusting flowers to the wind, birds to the season, also must be meritorious acts of giving. The principle testifying to King Ashoka's offering of half a mango to a group of hundreds of monks being great giving should also be studied well by those who receive. It is not only a matter of exerting physical effort; one should not miss the right opportunity.

Truly it is because the virtues of giving are inherent in oneself that one has now attained oneself. The Buddha said, "It may even be used oneself—how much the more can one give it to one's parents, spouse, and children." So we know that even using something oneself is a portion of giving; giving to one's parents, spouse, and children must also be giving. If one can give away even a mote of dust as charity, even though it is one's own doing, one should quietly rejoice in it, because one has correctly passed on one of the virtues of the Buddhas, because one has begun to practice one of the principles of bodhisattvas.

What is difficult to transform is the mind of living beings: this giving is to intend, from having put forth a single chattel and thus begun to transform the mind of living beings, to transform it even as far as attainment of enlightenment. In the beginning, it must be done by giving. For this reason in the beginning of the six transcendent ways is the transcendent way of giving. One should not calculate the greatness or smallness of the mind, nor the greatness or smallness of the thing. Nevertheless, there is a time when the mind transforms things, and there is giving in which things transform the mind.

Kind speech means that in looking upon living beings one should first arouse a mind of kindness and love and should utter caring, kind words. It is the absence of harsh speech. In ordinary social convention there is the etiquette of asking if someone is well or not; in Buddhism there is the expression "take care" and the ethical conduct of asking how someone is. To speak with the thought in one's heart of kindly minding living beings as one would a baby is kind speech.

Those with virtue one should praise; those without virtue one should pity. Once one has taken to kind speech, one will gradually increase kind speech; therefore hitherto unknown and unseen kind speech will appear. As long as one is alive now, one should gladly speak kindly; then one will never regress, life after life. The conquering of enemies and the harmonization of rulers is based on kind speech. To hear kind speech to one's face gladdens the countenance and pleases the heart; hearing kind speech indirectly makes a deep impression on the mind. You should know that kind speech comes from a kind heart, and a kind heart has good will as its seed. One should learn that kind speech has the power to turn the heavens. It is not just praising the able.

Beneficial action means to employ skills beneficial to living beings, high and low. For example, one watches over the road far and near, working out means to benefit others. One should pity even an exhausted turtle and take care of an ailing sparrow. When one has seen an exhausted turtle or an ailing sparrow, one doesn't want their thanks—one is simply moved to helpful action.

Fools think that when benefit to others is put first, one's own benefit will be reduced. It is not so. *Beneficial action* is one principle; it is universally benefiting self and others. An ancient ruler got out of the bath three times and spat out his food three times to go to the aid of others. He was not unwilling to educate the people of another country. So one should help equally those who are inimical and those who are friendly. It is to benefit self and others alike. If one acquires this heart, even in the plants and trees, wind and water, the principle of beneficial action being inherently nonregressive will indeed be beneficially acted out. One should wholeheartedly strive to rescue the ignorant.

Cooperation means nonopposition. It is not opposing oneself and not opposing others. It is like a human Buddha being the same as a human. Because of assimilation to the human world, we know a Buddha must assimilate to other worlds. When one knows cooperation, self and others are one thusness. Their music, song, and wine accompanies people, accompanies celestial beings, accompanies spirits. People keep company with music, song, and wine, and music, song, and wine keep company with music, song, and wine. People keep company with people, celestials keep company with celestials, spirits keep company with spirits—there is such logic. It is the learning of cooperation.

For example, a task of cooperation is a manner, is a standard, is an attitude. After regarding others as self, there must be a principle of assimilating oneself to others. Self and others are endless with time. An ancient philosopher said, "The ocean doesn't refuse water—therefore it has been able to become so immense. Mountains don't refuse earth—that is why they can be so high. An enlightened ruler doesn't refuse people—therefore his community can become populous." Know that the ocean's not refusing water is *cooperation*. Know further that the virtue of the water not refusing the ocean too is complete. For this reason water gathers and becomes an ocean, earth accumulates and becomes a mountain. We implicitly know that because the ocean doesn't refuse the ocean it forms an ocean and creates its immensity. Because the mountain doesn't refuse the mountain, it forms a mountain and makes its height. Because an enlightened ruler doesn't reject people, he forms a community of them. A sovereign does not reject people. Though the sovereign does not reject people, that does mean there are no rewards and punishments. But though there are rewards and punishments, there is no rejecting people.

In ancient times of pristine honesty, nations had no rewards or punishments. That is because the rewards and punishments of those times were not on a par with now. Even now there must be people who seek the right way even without reward. This is beyond the conception of the ignorant man. Because an enlightened ruler is wise, he doesn't reject people. People always form a nation—though they have a mind to seek an enlightened ruler, because there are few who thoroughly know the reason an enlightened ruler is an enlightened ruler, they only rejoice in not being rejected by an enlightened ruler but don't know how to not reject an enlightened ruler themselves. Therefore, because there is the logic of cooperation in both enlightened rulers and in ignorant people, cooperation is the practical undertaking of the bodhisattva. One should face everyone with a mild countenance.

1243

Birth and Death
(Shōji)

Birth and Death, which is undated in the *Shōbōgenzō,* integrates transcendence with being in the world. The theme is a reflection of the basic principle that existence is empty and emptiness is existence, which is put into practice by neither grasping nor rejecting, being free from both craving and aversion.

In a well-known Zen story a monk comes to a Zen master, who asks him where he has come from. "The South," replies the monk. The master asks the monk about Buddhism in the South, a region abounding in Zen centers; the monk answers, "There's a lot of discussion going on." The master says, "How can that compare with me planting the fields here and making rice balls to eat?" The monk, who apparently did not see anything enlightening or liberating about this, said, "What can you do about the world?" The master said, "What do you call the world?"

In the final analysis, according to the Zen teachings, it is not that the world binds people, it is people who bind themselves to the world. Bondage and delusion do not come from the world itself, but from ideas and attitudes regarding the world, from people's relation to the world. Therefore the question of what can be done about the world calls forth the question of what people think and feel the world to be.

Birth and Death

"Because there is Buddha in birth and death, there is no birth and death." Also, "because there is no Buddha in birth and death, one is not deluded by birth and death." These are the words of two Zen teachers called Kassan and Jōsan. Being the words of enlightened people, they were surely not uttered without reason. People who want to get out of birth and death should understand what they mean.

If people seek Buddha outside of birth and death, that is like heading north to go south, like facing south to try to see the north star: accumulating causes of birth and death all the more, they have lost the way to liberation. Simply understanding that birth and death is itself nirvana, there is nothing to reject as birth and death, nothing to seek as nirvana. Only then will one have some measure of detachment from birth and death.

It is a mistake to assume that one moves from birth to death. Birth, being one point in time, has a before and after; therefore in Buddhism birth is called unborn. Extinction too, being one point in time, also has before and after, so it is said that extinction is nonextinction. When we say "birth" there is nothing but birth, and when we say "extinction" there is nothing but extinction. Therefore when birth comes it is just birth, and when extinction comes it is just extinction. In facing birth and extinction, don't reject, don't long.

This birth and death is the life of the Buddha. If we try to reject or get rid of this, we would lose the life of the Buddha. If we linger in this and cling to birth and death, this too is losing the life of the Buddha; it is stopping the Buddha's manner of being. When we have no aversion or longing, only then do we reach the heart of the Buddha.

However, don't figure it in your mind, don't say it in words. Just letting go of and forgetting body and mind, casting them into the house of Buddha, being activated by the Buddha—when we go along in accord with this, then without applying effort or expending the mind we part from birth and death and become Buddhas. Who would linger in the mind?

There is a very easy way to become a Buddha: not doing any evil, having no attachment to birth and death, sympathizing deeply with all beings, respecting those above, sympathizing with those below, not feeling aversion or longing for anything, not thinking or worrying—this is called Buddha. Don't seek it anywhere else.

Production Notes

This book was designed by Roger Eggers.
Composition and paging were done on the
Quadex Composing System and typesetting on
the Compugraphic 8400 by the design and
production staff of University of Hawaii Press.

The text and display typeface is Sabon.

Offset presswork and binding were done by
Vail-Ballou Press, Inc. Text paper is Writers
RR Offset, basis 50.